The New
Heart of Wisdom

Also by Geshe Kelsang Gyatso

Meaningful to Behold
Clear Light of Bliss
Universal Compassion
Joyful Path of Good Fortune
The Bodhisattva Vow
Heart Jewel
Great Treasury of Merit
Introduction to Buddhism
Understanding the Mind
Tantric Grounds and Paths
Ocean of Nectar
Essence of Vajrayana
Living Meaningfully, Dying Joyfully
Eight Steps to Happiness
Transform Your Life
The New Meditation Handbook
How to Solve Our Human Problems
Mahamudra Tantra
Modern Buddhism
The New Guide to Dakini Land

Profits from the sale of this book are designated to the
NKT-IKBU International Temples Project Fund
according to the guidelines in *A Money Handbook*
[Reg. Charity number 1015054 (England)]
A Buddhist Charity, Building for World Peace
www.kadampa.org/temples

GESHE KELSANG GYATSO

The New
Heart of Wisdom

PROFOUND TEACHINGS FROM
BUDDHA'S HEART

THARPA PUBLICATIONS
UK • US • CANADA
AUSTRALIA • ASIA

First published as *Heart of Wisdom* 1986.
Second edition published as *Heart of Wisdom* 1989.
Third edition revised and reset 1996.
Fourth edition published as *Heart of Wisdom*
with new line illustrations and reset 2001.
Reprinted 2004, 2005, 2008, 2010.
Fifth edition substantially revised and published as
The New Heart of Wisdom 2012. Reprinted 2013

Tharpa Publications UK Office
Conishead Priory
Ulverston, Cumbria
LA12 9QQ, England

Tharpa Publications US Office
47 Sweeney Road
Glen Spey
NY 12737, USA

Tharpa Publications has offices around the world,
and Tharpa books are published in most major languages.
See page 327 for contact details.

The cover image is Great Mother Prajnaparamita

Library of Congress Control Number: 2012939185

British Library Cataloguing in Publication Data
A catalogue record for this book is
available from the British Library.

ISBN 978-1-906665-05-0 – hardback
ISBN 978-1-906665-04-3 – paperback
ISBN 978-1-906665-16-6 – e-book
ISBN 978-1-906665-17-3 – Adobe Portable Document format (.pdf)

Set in Palatino by Tharpa Publications.
Printed on Munken Pure by
CPI Group (UK) Ltd., Croydon, CR0 4YY

Paper supplied from well-managed forests and other controlled
sources, and certified in accordance with the rules of the
Forest Stewardship Council.

Contents

Illustrations

Buddha Shakyamuni

Introduction

I feel very fortunate to have the opportunity to give this commentary to the *Essence of Wisdom Sutra*, or *Heart Sutra*. Similarly, those who have the opportunity to study the meaning of this Sutra, which is the essence of Buddha's teachings, are also extremely fortunate. Because of the profound nature of this Sutra it is possible that some people will find certain parts of this commentary difficult to understand. I will try to explain it as clearly as possible, to the limit of my ability, but because this Sutra reveals Buddha's ultimate view and intention, we must be prepared to encounter some difficulties. Please do not become discouraged: through patient study with effort we will gain a clear understanding of the entire Sutra. As our familiarity with these teachings grows, so too will our understanding.

All Buddha's teachings are either Sutra, the common teachings, or Tantra, the uncommon teachings; there is not a single scripture of Buddha that is not one of these two. Sutra teachings are divided into two types: Hinayana Sutras and Mahayana Sutras. Of these, the *Essence of Wisdom Sutra* belongs to the category of Mahayana Sutras. The Mahayana Sutras themselves comprise many different types of teaching, but the most precious and supreme are the *Perfection of Wisdom Sutras* (Skt. *Prajnaparamitasutra*). Buddha's ultimate intention is to lead each and every living being to the supreme happiness of enlightenment by showing

1

them the Mahayana path. For this purpose he taught the *Perfection of Wisdom Sutras*.

There are several *Perfection of Wisdom Sutras* of varying lengths. The most extensive is the *Perfection of Wisdom Sutra in One Hundred Thousand Lines*, which in the Tibetan translation occupies twelve volumes. There is also a medium length Sutra of twenty-five thousand lines in three volumes, and a short, single-volume Sutra of eight thousand lines. In addition, there is an even shorter Sutra in eight chapters of verse known as the *Condensed Perfection of Wisdom Sutra*. The *Perfection of Wisdom Sutras* explain all the stages of the paths of wisdom and method. 'Wisdom' refers to a realization that releases our Buddha nature from obstructions, and 'method' refers to a realization that ripens our Buddha nature. In particular, in these Sutras Buddha reveals his ultimate view and intention, and thus among Sutras the *Perfection of Wisdom Sutras* are held to be supreme.

The *Essence of Wisdom Sutra* is much shorter than the other *Perfection of Wisdom Sutras* but it contains explicitly or implicitly the entire meaning of the longer Sutras. It is because it contains the very essence of the perfection of wisdom teachings that it is known as the *Essence of Wisdom Sutra*. Through the study and practice of this Sutra we can gain a perfect understanding of the ultimate nature of all phenomena, overcome hindrances and difficulties in our daily life, and finally overcome the obstacles preventing our full awakening and thereby attain the enlightened state of a Buddha. We are indeed fortunate to have met these essential teachings of Buddha.

The subject matter of these teachings is training in the perfection of wisdom. Wisdom is a virtuous intelligent mind whose function is to dispel the inner darkness of ignorance.

With wisdom we can know how things really are. Normally we do not understand the real nature of things; nor do we understand that suffering comes from non-virtuous actions and happiness from virtuous actions. All this is ignorance. Because of this lack of understanding, even though we do not want to suffer we create our own suffering by performing non-virtuous actions. And although we want to be happy all the time, we destroy our own happiness by developing anger, negative views and wrong intentions. We should know that this is our normal situation.

All our suffering and problems come from our ignorance, and because of ignorance we have experienced suffering and problems in life after life, since beginningless time until this life. Now is the time to abandon ignorance permanently, while we have the precious opportunity to listen to and practise Buddhadharma. The only method to abandon our ignorance and attain the supreme happiness of enlightenment is to accomplish the realization of the perfection of wisdom in general, and especially the realization of the higher perfection of wisdom.

The perfection of wisdom is wisdom that is associated with the mind of compassion for all living beings. This wisdom enables us to gain victory over maras – the outer and inner obstructing demons – and become a fully enlightened being like Buddha Shakyamuni. How wonderful!

Commentary to the *Heart Sutra*

PART ONE:
THE EXPLANATION OF THE DIRECT MEANING OF THE SUTRA

Great Mother Prajnaparamita

The Title and Homage

The explanation of the direct meaning of the Sutra is presented under the following three main headings:

1 The meaning of the title
2 The homage of the translators
3 The explanation of the main body of the Sutra

THE MEANING OF THE TITLE

Essence of the perfection of wisdom, the Blessed Mother

This is a translation of the title of the Sutra into English. In the Tibetan text the title is given first in Sanskrit and then in Tibetan, as follows:

Sanskrit: *Bhagavatiprajnaparamitahrdaya*
Tibetan: *Chom den de ma she rab kyi pa rol tu jin pai nying po*

The essence of the perfection of wisdom is a wisdom that realizes emptiness directly, associated with the compassionate mind of bodhichitta. With this wisdom, in one single concentration, we can accumulate a great collection of merit and a great collection of wisdom, the main causes of Buddha's Form Body and Truth Body, respectively. This wisdom will lead us to the attainment of full enlightenment very quickly. It is called the 'Blessed Mother' because all the Buddhas of the ten directions are born from this wisdom. In summary, the actual essence of the perfection of wisdom, the Blessed Mother, is a wisdom that realizes emptiness directly, associated with the compassionate mind of bodhichitta. It is known as 'ultimate bodhichitta'.

Because this Sutra teaches us how to accomplish this wisdom it is called *Essence of the Perfection of Wisdom, the Blessed Mother*, indicating that we can accomplish the essence of the perfection of wisdom, the Blessed Mother, through the study and practice of this Sutra. This is similar to Nagarjuna's text *Fundamental Wisdom* being called *Middle Way* (Tib. *Uma*): although the actual middle way is emptiness, this text is called *Middle Way* because it teaches us how to train in emptiness.

As mentioned before, in general, wisdom is a virtuous intelligent mind whose function is to dispel the inner darkness of ignorance. With wisdom we can understand profound objects such as how things really exist, subtle dependent-related phenomena, and karma – the relationship between the actions of our former lives and the experiences of our present life, and between the actions of our present life and the experiences of our future lives. This knowledge gives us permanent liberation from suffering and makes our human life meaningful.

Many people are very intelligent in accomplishing worldly attainments. This intelligence is not wisdom because worldly attainments such as a high position, reputation, wealth and success in business are deceptive. If we die tomorrow, they will disappear tomorrow, and nothing will be left for our future. Wisdom, however, will never deceive us. It is our inner Spiritual Guide, who leads us to the correct path. It is the divine eye through which we can see what we should know, what we should abandon, what we should practise and what we should attain. We should know that because of lacking wisdom we have wasted our countless former lives without any meaning. When we take birth as a human being in this world, we bring nothing with us from our former lives except suffering and delusions. Out of his compassion, Buddha gave teachings on the perfection of wisdom to liberate all living beings from suffering. Of all wisdoms, the perfection of wisdom of ultimate bodhichitta is supreme. We can accomplish this wisdom through the sincere study and practice of this Sutra.

THE HOMAGE OF THE TRANSLATORS

Homage to the perfection of wisdom, the Blessed Mother.

In this context, the perfection of wisdom, the Blessed Mother, refers to the female enlightened being, Great Mother Prajnaparamita, who is the manifestation of the perfection of wisdom of all the Buddhas of the ten directions. When this Sutra was translated from Sanskrit into Tibetan the translators made a special prayer to Great Mother Prajnaparamita to pacify obstacles and to spread the teachings of this precious Sutra. We should deeply rejoice in the excellent deeds of these translators and recognize their great kindness to us. Without their efforts in translating this Sutra, both Tibetans and Westerners would have no basis to listen to this precious Sutra, let alone study and practise it. How kind these translators are for us! Perhaps they are emanations of Buddha himself. It is our responsibility to repay their kindness by sincerely studying and practising this precious holy Dharma so that we can fulfil our own as well as others' wishes.

The Background and Shariputra's Question

THE EXPLANATION OF THE MAIN BODY OF THE SUTRA

This explanation is given under the following three main headings:

1 The common explanation of the background to the Sutra
2 The uncommon explanation of the background to the Sutra
3 The explanation of the actual Sutra

THE COMMON EXPLANATION OF THE
BACKGROUND TO THE SUTRA

Thus I have heard. At one time the Blessed One was dwelling in Rajagriha on Massed Vultures Mountain together with a great assembly of monks and nuns, and a great assembly of Bodhisattvas.

This part of the explanation of the background to the Sutra is called the 'common explanation' because it deals with aspects of the background that are easily understood and were commonly known by those present.

'Thus I have heard' indicates that this part of the text was explicitly spoken by Ananda, who was a close disciple of Buddha. After Buddha passed away, it was principally Ananda who collected Buddha's words and passed on his teachings to others. Although the explanation of the background was not spoken by Buddha, these words are nevertheless considered to be the word of Buddha because Buddha himself blessed the mental continuum of Ananda and gave him permission to say this.

At the beginning of more extensive Sutras it is the general practice to present a detailed background of the Sutra. In this case, the background is greatly abbreviated, but nevertheless contains the following four points:

1 The speaker of the Sutra
2 The time when the Sutra was delivered
3 The place where the Sutra was delivered
4 To whom the Sutra was spoken

THE SPEAKER OF THE SUTRA

'The Blessed One' here refers to Buddha Shakyamuni. It was he who effectively delivered this Sutra, as will be explained later.

It is very inspiring to contemplate the life story of Buddha and his excellent deeds. In general, 'Buddha' means 'Awakened One', someone who has awakened from the sleep of ignorance and sees things as they really are. A Buddha is a person who is completely free from all faults and mental obstructions. There are many people who have become

Buddhas in the past, and all living beings will become Buddhas in the future.

The Buddha who is the founder of the Buddhist religion is called Buddha Shakyamuni. 'Shakya' is the name of the royal family into which he was born, and 'Muni' means 'Able One'. Buddha Shakyamuni was born as a royal prince in 624 BC in a place called Lumbini, in what is now Nepal. His mother's name was Queen Mayadevi and his father's name was King Shuddhodana.

One night, Queen Mayadevi dreamed that a white elephant descended from heaven and entered her womb. The white elephant entering her womb indicated that on that very night she had conceived a child who was a pure and powerful being. The elephant descending from heaven indicated that her child came from Tushita heaven, the Pure Land of Buddha Maitreya. Later, when she gave birth to the child, instead of experiencing pain the queen experienced a special, pure vision in which she stood holding the branch of a tree with her right hand while the gods Brahma and Indra took the child painlessly from her side. They then proceeded to honour the infant by offering him ritual ablutions.

When the king saw the child he felt as if all his wishes had been fulfilled and he named the young prince 'Siddhartha'. He invited a Brahmin seer to make predictions about the prince's future. The seer examined the child with his clairvoyance and told the king, 'There are signs that the boy could become either a chakravatin king – a ruler of the entire world – or a fully enlightened Buddha. However, since the time for chakravatin kings is now past, it is certain that he will become a Buddha and that his beneficial influence will pervade the thousand million worlds like the rays of a sun.'

Avalokiteshvara

As the young prince grew up, he mastered all the traditional arts and sciences without needing any instruction. He knew sixty-four different languages, each with its own alphabet, and he was also very skilled at mathematics. He once told his father that he could count all the atoms in the world in the time it takes to draw a single breath. Although he did not need to study, he did so to please his father and to benefit others. At his father's request, he joined a school where, in addition to studying various academic subjects, he became skilled at sports such as martial arts and archery. The prince would take every opportunity to convey spiritual meanings and to encourage others to follow spiritual paths. At one time, when he was taking part in an archery contest, he declared, 'With the bow of meditative concentration I will fire the arrow of wisdom and kill the tiger of ignorance in living beings.' He then released the arrow and it flew straight through five iron tigers and seven trees before disappearing into the earth! By witnessing demonstrations such as this, thousands of people developed faith in the prince.

Sometimes Prince Siddhartha would go into the capital city of his father's kingdom to see how the people lived. During these visits, he came into contact with many old and sick people, and on one occasion he saw a corpse. These encounters left a deep impression on his mind and led him to realize that all living beings without exception have to experience the sufferings of birth, sickness, ageing and death. Because he understood the laws of rebirth, he also realized that living beings experience these sufferings not just once, but again and again, in life after life without cessation. Seeing how all living beings are trapped in this vicious cycle of suffering he felt deep compassion for them and developed a sincere wish to free all of them from their suffering. Realizing that only a fully enlightened Buddha has the wisdom and power to help all living beings in this way, he resolved to leave the palace and retire to the solitude of the forest where he would engage in profound meditation until he attained enlightenment.

When the people of the Shakya kingdom realized that the prince intended to leave the palace they requested the king to arrange a marriage for him in the hope that this would cause him to change his mind. The king agreed and soon found him a suitable bride, Yasodhara, the daughter of a respected Shakya family. Prince Siddhartha, however, had no attachment to worldly pleasures because he realized that objects of attachment are like poisonous flowers, which initially appear to be attractive but eventually give rise to great pain. His resolve to leave the palace and attain enlightenment remained unchanged, but to fulfil his father's wishes, and to bring temporary benefit to the Shakya people, he agreed to marry Yasodhara. However, even though he remained in the palace as a royal prince, he devoted all his time and energy to serving the Shakya people in whatever way he could.

When he was twenty-nine years old, the prince had a vision in which all the Buddhas of the ten directions appeared to him and spoke in unison, saying, 'Previously you resolved to become a Conqueror Buddha so that you could help all living beings trapped in the cycle of suffering. Now is the time for you to accomplish this.' The prince went immediately to his parents and told them of his intention: 'I wish to retire to a peaceful place in the forest where I can engage in deep meditation and quickly attain full enlightenment. Once I have attained enlightenment, I will be able to repay the kindness of all living beings, and especially the great kindness that you have shown me. Therefore, I request your permission to leave the palace.' When his parents heard this, they were shocked, and the king refused to grant his permission. Prince Siddhartha said to his father, 'Father, if you can give me permanent freedom from the sufferings of birth, sickness, ageing and death I will stay in the palace; but if you cannot I must leave and make my human life meaningful.'

The king tried all means to prevent his son from leaving the palace. In the hope that the prince might change his mind, he surrounded him with a retinue of beautiful women, dancers, singers and musicians, who day and night used their charms to please him. In case the prince might attempt a secret escape, he posted guards around the palace walls. However, the prince's determination to leave the palace and enter a life of meditation could not be shaken. One night he used his miracle powers to send the guards and attendants into a deep sleep while he made his escape from the palace with the help of a trusted aide. After they had travelled about six miles, the prince dismounted from his horse and bade farewell to his aide. He then cut off his hair and threw it into the sky, where it was caught by the gods of the Land of the Thirty-three Heavens. One of the gods then offered the prince the saffron robes of a religious mendicant. The prince accepted these and gave his royal garments to the god in exchange. In this way, he ordained himself as a monk.

Siddhartha then made his way to a place near Bodh Gaya in India, where he found a suitable site for meditation. There he remained, emphasizing a meditation called 'space-like concentration on the Dharmakaya', in which he focused single-pointedly on the ultimate nature of all phenomena. After training in this meditation for six years he realized he was very close to attaining full enlightenment, and so he walked to Bodh Gaya where, on the fifteenth day of the fourth month, he seated himself beneath the Bodhi Tree in the meditation posture and vowed not to rise from meditation until he had attained perfect enlightenment. With this determination, he entered the space-like concentration on the Dharmakaya.

As dusk fell, Devaputra Mara, the chief of all the demons, or maras, in this world, tried to disturb Siddhartha's concentration by conjuring up many fearful apparitions. He manifested hosts of terrifying demons – some throwing spears, some firing arrows, some trying to burn him with fire, and some hurling boulders and even mountains at him. Siddhartha, however, remained completely undisturbed. Through the force of his concentration, the weapons, rocks and mountains appeared to him as a rain of fragrant flowers, and the raging fires became like offerings of rainbow light.

Seeing that Siddhartha could not be frightened into abandoning his meditation, Devaputra Mara tried instead to distract him by manifesting countless beautiful women, but Siddhartha responded by developing even deeper concentration. In this way he triumphed over all the demons of this world, which is why he subsequently became known as a 'Conqueror Buddha'.

Siddhartha then continued with his meditation until dawn, when he attained the 'vajra-like concentration'. With this concentration, which is the very last mind of a limited being, he removed the final veils of ignorance from his mind and in the next moment became a Buddha, a fully enlightened being.

There is nothing that Buddha does not know. Because he has woken from the sleep of ignorance and has removed all obstructions from his mind, he knows everything of the past, present and future, directly and simultaneously. Moreover, Buddha has great compassion that is completely impartial, embracing all living beings without discrimination. He benefits all living beings without exception by emanating various forms throughout the universe and by bestowing his blessings on their minds. Through receiving Buddha's blessings, all beings, even the lowliest animals, sometimes develop peaceful and virtuous states of mind. Eventually, through meeting an emanation of Buddha in the form of a Spiritual Guide, everyone will have the opportunity to enter the path to liberation and enlightenment. As the great Indian Buddhist scholar Nagarjuna said, there is no one who has not received help from Buddha.

Forty-nine days after Buddha attained enlightenment, the gods Brahma and Indra requested him to teach, saying:

> O Buddha, Treasure of Compassion,
> Living beings are like blind people, in constant danger
>   of falling into the lower realms.
> Other than you there is no Protector in this world.
> Therefore we beseech you, please rise from meditative
>   equipoise and turn the Wheel of Dharma.

As a result of this request, Buddha rose from meditation and taught the first Wheel of Dharma. These teachings, which include the *Sutra of the Four Noble Truths* and other discourses, are the principal source of the Hinayana, or Lesser Vehicle, of Buddhism. Later, Buddha taught the second and third Wheels of Dharma, which include the *Perfection of Wisdom Sutras* and the *Sutra Discriminating the Intention*, respectively. These teachings are the source of the Mahayana, or Great Vehicle, of Buddhism. In the Hinayana teachings, Buddha explains how to attain liberation from suffering for oneself alone. In the Mahayana teachings, he explains how to attain full enlightenment, or Buddhahood, for the sake of others. Both traditions flourished in Asia, at first in India and then gradually in other surrounding countries, including Tibet. Now they are also beginning to flourish in countries throughout the world.

The reason why Buddha's teachings are called the 'Wheel of Dharma' is as follows. It is said that in ancient times there were great kings, known as 'chakravatin kings', who used to rule the entire world. These kings had many special possessions, including a precious wheel in which they would travel around the world. Wherever the precious wheel went, the king would control that region. Buddha's teachings are said to be like a precious wheel because wherever they spread the people in that area have the opportunity to control their delusions by putting these teachings into practice.

'Dharma' means 'protection'. By practising Buddha's teachings we protect ourself from suffering and problems. All the problems we experience during daily life originate in ignorance, and the method for eliminating ignorance is to practise Dharma.

Practising Dharma is the supreme method for improving the quality of our human life. The quality of life depends not on external development or material progress, but on the inner development of peace and happiness. For example, in the past many Buddhists lived in poor and underdeveloped countries, but they were able to find pure, lasting happiness by practising what Buddha had taught.

If we integrate Buddha's teachings into our daily life, we will be able to solve all our inner problems and attain a truly peaceful mind. Without inner peace, outer peace is impossible. If we first establish peace within our minds by training in spiritual paths, outer peace will come naturally; but if we do not, world peace will never be achieved, no matter how many people campaign for it.

THE TIME WHEN THE SUTRA WAS DELIVERED

'At one time' refers to the period after Buddha had travelled to Rajagriha from Vaishali, having given a demonstration of his extensive miracle powers. Buddha was therefore about fifty-seven years old when he delivered this Sutra.

THE PLACE WHERE THE SUTRA WAS DELIVERED

'Was dwelling in Rajagriha on Massed Vultures Mountain': this Sutra, as well as the longer *Perfection of Wisdom Sutras*, was delivered while Buddha Shakyamuni was staying near Rajagriha, which is in the present day Bihar province of India, quite near to Bodh Gaya. The precise location of the discourse was a mountain known as 'Massed Vultures Mountain' (Skt. *Gridhrakutaparvata*).

When Buddha was expounding the *Perfection of Wisdom Sutras*, many Bodhisattvas from various world systems came to listen, manifesting in the form of vultures. To the eyes of ordinary people it appeared that the mountain was covered in a vast flock of vultures, and as a result the mountain became known as 'Massed Vultures Mountain'. This is one of several interpretations of the origin of this name.

TO WHOM THE SUTRA WAS SPOKEN

'Together with a great assembly of monks and nuns, and a great assembly of Bodhisattvas': since Buddha was giving Mahayana discourses during his time on Massed Vultures

Mountain, his circle of followers included not only a great number of monks, such as Shariputra and Subhuti, and nuns, but also a great number of Bodhisattvas, such as Avalokiteshvara and Maitreya. A great number of gods, demi-gods, nagas and spirits were also present.

THE UNCOMMON EXPLANATION OF THE BACKGROUND TO THE SUTRA

At that time the Blessed One was absorbed in the concentration of the countless aspects of phenomena, called 'Profound Illumination'.

At that time also the Superior Avalokiteshvara, the Bodhisattva, the Great Being, was looking perfectly at the practice of the profound perfection of wisdom, looking perfectly also at the five aggregates being empty of inherent existence.

This part of the explanation of the background to the Sutra is called the 'uncommon explanation' because it explains aspects of the circumstances of the Sutra that were not commonly known by those present.

At the time of the Sutra, which was during his stay on Massed Vultures Mountain, Buddha was absorbed in a state of meditative concentration on the direct realization of the union of the two truths – the union of profound emptiness and illumination, the mere appearance of the countless aspects of all phenomena. This is an uncommon, supreme quality of Buddha.

This meditative concentration is also called 'Profound Illumination' because, while Buddha's mind was focused single-pointedly on the profound object, the union of the two truths, his body radiated a vast amount of brilliant light, filling the entire world. The light purified the environment and living beings' minds, and caused the seeds of the paths to liberation and full enlightenment to ripen in their minds. Only those beings with sufficiently pure minds were able to perceive that Buddha was engaged in these deeds and emanating light in this way. This is why this part of the background is included in the uncommon explanation.

There was another reason why Buddha radiated light in this way. When profound discourses such as the *Perfection of Wisdom Sutras* were being given, a vast host of gods from the desire and form realms also came to listen. These gods have bodies that radiate light, and from their point of view humans are stunted, bad-smelling and toad-like. Therefore, when these celestial beings took their places about Massed Vultures Mountain, their minds were filled with haughtiness and pride. Having such pride is a great obstacle to receiving benefit from spiritual teachings and so to deflate their pride Buddha radiated brilliant light from his own body. His body outshone those of the gods as the sun outshines the light of fireflies. Through this display, the gods were humbled and their minds became receptive to Buddha's teachings.

While Buddha was absorbed in concentration, Avalokiteshvara was meditating on the profound view of emptiness. In the text, it states specifically that Avalokiteshvara was observing how the five aggregates – form, feeling, discrimination, compositional factors and consciousness – are empty of inherent existence, but the presence of the word 'also' implies that Avalokiteshvara had also looked at the emptiness of the self, or person. The meaning of 'empty of inherent existence' will be explained in the next chapter.

Manjushri

The special qualities of Avalokiteshvara are indicated by the references to him as 'the Superior Avalokiteshvara, the Bodhisattva, the Great Being'. He is given the title 'Superior' because he has realized emptiness directly and is thus a Superior being. Avalokiteshvara is also a Bodhisattva, a person who is spontaneously motivated by the mind of bodhichitta. Someone who has developed this motivation has thereby entered the Mahayana path. Bodhichitta has two principal aspirations: the wish to benefit and bring happiness to all living beings without exception, and the wish to attain the state of Buddhahood in order to be most able to accomplish the first aspiration. A Bodhisattva is therefore someone who is principally motivated by these two wishes. Avalokiteshvara is worthy to be called a 'Great Being' because, being a Bodhisattva, he works with great courage and energy solely for the benefit and welfare of others.

Although he assumed the form of a Bodhisattva disciple of Buddha Shakyamuni, Avalokiteshvara had already attained full enlightenment many aeons previously. The same is also true of Manjushri, Vajrapani, Samantabhadra, Maitreya and the other principal Mahayana disciples of Buddha Shakyamuni. Although they were in essence Buddhas themselves, they demonstrated the correct manner of being Bodhisattva disciples and helped to spread the teachings of Buddha Shakyamuni in order to benefit others extensively.

THE EXPLANATION OF THE ACTUAL SUTRA

The part of the text considered so far, giving the background to the actual discourse, is omitted from some shorter versions of the Sutra. The remaining part of the text contains the actual Sutra and is explained in four parts:

THE QUESTION OF SHARIPUTRA

Then, through the power of Buddha, the Venerable Shariputra said to the Superior Avalokiteshvara, the Bodhisattva, the Great Being, 'How should a Son of the lineage train who wishes to engage in the practice of the profound perfection of wisdom?'

This part of the Sutra consists of a question by Shariputra addressed to Avalokiteshvara. While Buddha was absorbed in the meditative concentration called 'Profound Illumination' he blessed the minds of Shariputra and Avalokiteshvara so that Shariputra was inspired to ask his question and Avalokiteshvara was inspired to give his answers. Therefore, since both disciples spoke through the power and inspiration of Buddha, the entire Sutra is correctly considered to be the word of Buddha.

If something is the word of Buddha, it is not necessarily spoken through his mouth. Buddha taught this Sutra through his heart, not through his mouth. For example, in some Sutras Buddha gave teachings through his crown protrusion, and in one Sutra, through the power of Buddha, even the wind moving the branches of a tree gave rise to words of Dharma. Those Sutras, as well as this present Sutra, are the authentic word of Buddha because they arose through Buddha's power and inspiration.

Shariputra was one of the main disciples of Buddha Shakyamuni, having a very special relationship with him from previous lives. From the point of view of ordinary appearances, he was a Hearer Foe Destroyer of the Hinayana lineage. A 'Foe Destroyer' is someone who has destroyed the inner enemy of delusions.

In Shariputra's question, 'Son of the lineage' refers to someone who has entered the Mahayana lineage. A person enters the Mahayana lineage by developing the mind of compassion for all living beings, so Shariputra is referring to someone who has cultivated this compassion. Although Shariputra refers only to 'Son of the lineage' in his question, 'Daughter of the lineage' is also implied and is expressed explicitly in the answer given by Avalokiteshvara. Indeed, some texts also contain the word 'Daughter' at this point.

Here, the words 'the practice of the profound perfection of wisdom' reveal that training in the perfection of wisdom and emptiness is very profound. It is the very essence of Buddha's teachings. Training in this wisdom and emptiness will finally lead all living beings to the supreme happiness of full enlightenment. As mentioned before, the perfection of wisdom is a wisdom that realizes emptiness, the way things really are, associated with the compassionate mind of bodhichitta.

Therefore, the meaning of Shariputra's question is, 'How should those beings train who have entered the Mahayana lineage by developing compassion for all living beings and wish to engage in the profound practice of the perfection of wisdom and emptiness?'

Vajrapani

The Paths of Accumulation and Preparation (1)

Avalokiteshvara's answers to Shariputra's question explain how to train in the perfection of wisdom in relation to the five Mahayana paths. Therefore, at this point it will be helpful to consider the meaning of paths in general and the five Mahayana paths in particular.

We are all familiar with external paths. These lead from one external place to another, and we can easily understand them by consulting maps and so forth. Internal paths, on the other hand, are types of mind and are much more difficult to understand. Although internal paths are minds, or actions of mind, they are called 'paths' because they lead us to experience happiness, suffering, or neutral feelings. Those types of mind that lead to rebirth in samsara are mundane paths. Some of these paths are non-virtuous, leading to rebirth in the three lower realms – the animal, hungry ghost and hell realms – and others are virtuous, leading to rebirth in the three higher realms – the human, demi-god and god realms. Taking a contaminated body and mind in life after life within any of these six realms is samsara.

We should know that of the three types of action – actions of body, speech and mind – mental actions are the most important. This is because physical and verbal actions depend upon motivation, which is a mental action. When our mind makes a determination to do something, this determination is an action of mind, and is called 'karma'. If this determination is virtuous or positive it will be a virtuous action or karma, which will lead us to a state of happiness. If the determination is non-virtuous or negative it will be a non-virtuous action, which will lead us to a state of suffering.

All meditations are virtuous actions of mind. When we are meditating we are performing a virtuous mental action. When we are angry and make the determination to harm others we are performing a non-virtuous mental action. Actions of mind are much more powerful than actions of body and speech. They are called 'internal paths' because they lead us to experience happiness, suffering, or neutral feelings in the future.

Actions of mind that lead to permanent liberation from samsara, such as meditations motivated by renunciation, are supramundane paths. They can be divided into Hinayana paths, which lead to personal liberation, and Mahayana paths, which lead to the full enlightenment of Buddhahood. Hinayana paths are the five paths of the Solitary Conqueror and the five paths of the Hearer. Similarly, there are five Mahayana paths – the Mahayana paths of accumulation, preparation, seeing, meditation and No More Learning. These five Mahayana paths are minds that lead progressively to the attainment of full enlightenment – the fifth Mahayana path being the fully enlightened mind itself. The way to enter the Mahayana paths and to progress from path to path is as follows.

The moment we develop the supreme good heart of bodhichitta we enter the Mahayana path and the Bodhisattva's path, and we become a Bodhisattva on the path of accumulation. A Bodhisattva is a person who sincerely seeks the attainment of enlightenment, motivated by compassion for all living beings. Bodhichitta is the spontaneous wish to attain enlightenment to benefit each and every living being directly.

The initial bodhichitta itself, and all other realizations associated with this initial bodhichitta, are called the 'Mahayana path of accumulation' because at this stage the Bodhisattva emphasizes accumulating a great collection of wisdom by training in the concentration of tranquil abiding observing emptiness. By doing this, when through the power of the concentration of tranquil abiding the Bodhisattva experiences a special wisdom called 'superior seeing' that realizes the emptiness of all phenomena very clearly, he or she advances from the path of accumulation to the path of preparation and becomes a Bodhisattva on the path of preparation.

This Bodhisattva's initial realization of superior seeing observing emptiness, and all other realizations associated with this initial superior seeing, are called the 'Mahayana path of preparation' because at this stage the Bodhisattva emphasizes preparing to realize directly the emptiness of all phenomena by continually meditating on emptiness with the union of tranquil abiding and superior seeing.

By doing this, when his or her wisdom of superior seeing directly realizes the emptiness of all phenomena, the Bodhisattva advances from the path of preparation to the path of seeing and becomes a Bodhisattva on the path of seeing. This Bodhisattva's initial direct realization of emptiness, and all other realizations associated with this initial direct realization of emptiness, are called the 'Mahayana path of seeing' because it is the first time that the Bodhisattva directly sees emptiness, the way things really are. At this stage he or she becomes a Superior Bodhisattva and no longer experiences any physical or mental pain. Even if his or her body is cut piece by piece with a knife the Bodhisattva feels no pain because he realizes directly that there is no body other than emptiness.

Having attained the Mahayana path of seeing, to reach directly the final destination, the state of full enlightenment, the Bodhisattva continues to engage in meditation on emptiness. When he or she advances from the path of seeing to the path of meditation he becomes a Bodhisattva on the path of meditation. The realization of this Bodhisattva is called the 'path of meditation' because it indicates that the realization of this meditation is the last 'station' from which he will directly reach the final destination of enlightenment.

Through continually progressing on the Mahayana path of meditation the Bodhisattva will experience the advanced realization called the 'vajra-like-concentration', which has the power to remove the subtle mistaken appearance of all phenomena from his or her mind. In the next moment his subtle mistaken appearance of all phenomena will cease permanently and he will become an enlightened Buddha. A clear explanation about subtle mistaken appearance can be found in the book *Modern Buddhism*.

Actual enlightenment is Buddha's omniscient wisdom, which is free from subtle mistaken appearance of all phenomena and has the power to bestow peace of mind on each and every living being. It is also called the 'Mahayana Path of No More Learning'.

Avalokiteshvara's explanation of how to train in the perfection of wisdom in relation to the five Mahayana paths has six parts:

1 A brief explanation of how to train in the perfection of wisdom on the paths of accumulation and preparation
2 An extensive explanation of how to train in the perfection of wisdom on the paths of accumulation and preparation
3 An explanation of how to train in the perfection of wisdom on the path of seeing
4 An explanation of how to train in the perfection of wisdom on the path of meditation
5 An explanation of how to attain the Path of No More Learning
6 Conclusion

A BRIEF EXPLANATION OF HOW TO TRAIN IN THE PERFECTION OF WISDOM ON THE PATHS OF ACCUMULATION AND PREPARATION

Thus he spoke, and the Superior Avalokiteshvara, the Bodhisattva, the Great Being, replied to the Venerable Shariputra as follows:

'Shariputra, whatever Son or Daughter of the lineage wishes to engage in the practice of the profound perfection of wisdom should look perfectly like this: subsequently looking perfectly and correctly also at the five aggregates being empty of inherent existence.'

Maitreya

Avalokiteshvara's answer directly and indirectly contains the following advice. Practitioners, both male and female, who have entered the Mahayana lineage and wish to train in the profound practice of the perfection of wisdom should first look, or understand, with a subsequent valid cognizer that their own I or self is empty of, or lacks, inherent existence. Then, they should look, or understand, that their five aggregates also are empty of inherent existence. Having understood this, practitioners motivated by compassion for all living beings should meditate on the selflessness of the person, the mere absence of their own I or self existing inherently, and also meditate on the selflessness of phenomena, the mere absence of their five aggregates existing inherently. In this way, such practitioners should train in the perfection of wisdom perfectly and correctly.

Only Bodhisattvas on the path of accumulation or the path of preparation realize emptiness with a subsequent valid cognizer. Bodhisattvas on the path of seeing and on the path of meditation do not need to rely on a subsequent valid cognizer to understand emptiness because they realize emptiness with a direct valid cognizer. From this we can understand that this part of the Sutra explains how to train in the perfection of wisdom and emptiness in relation to the Mahayana paths of accumulation and preparation.

Here the word 'subsequently' has great meaning. It indicates that the mind with which we should first understand emptiness is a subsequent valid cognizer. A valid cognizer is a mind that realizes its object non-deceptively. Such a mind will never deceive us with respect to the object it ascertains. There are two types of valid cognizer: subsequent valid cognizers and direct valid cognizers. They are distinguished by the fact that a subsequent valid cognizer relies upon a sign, or reason, to know its object, whereas a direct valid cognizer knows its object directly without the need to rely upon a reason.

We have a lot of experience of direct valid cognizers, as this category of mind includes all valid sense consciousnesses. For example, the eye consciousness that correctly ascertains this book is a direct valid cognizer because it ascertains the book directly without relying upon reasoning. Subsequent valid cognizers are less common, but they are an important type of understanding. We can consider a simple example. When we see smoke rising from the chimney of a house we may develop the certainty that a fire has been lit in that house. We cannot see the fire directly but, using the presence of the smoke as a sign, or reason, we know without a doubt that there is (or has been) a fire there. Therefore, the presence of smoke is a correct sign indicating the existence of fire, and the mind that realizes the existence of fire in dependence upon this sign is a subsequent valid cognizer. Also, we can sometimes know that a person is unhappy by seeing him or her crying. Although we cannot see the person's state of mind directly, we develop a subsequent valid cognizer that knows the person is unhappy by using the outward behaviour as a sign. Since a subsequent valid cognizer depends upon a reason, we must first develop a realization of the reason. Then we can generate a subsequent valid cognizer. It is called a 'subsequent valid cognizer' because it realizes its object after understanding a valid reason.

Not all minds are valid cognizers because not all minds know their object non-deceptively. For example, a tree stump at dusk may appear to our eye consciousness as a person, but this mind is not a valid mind and deceives us. Also a child may develop the thought that certain berries are good to eat because they are black and shiny. This thought is similar to a subsequent cognizer but it is not a valid mind because the reason used is not correct. The resulting mind is deceptive and could even lead to the child's death.

If we wish to gain faultless knowledge of a phenomenon we must know that phenomenon with a valid cognizer. There are many phenomena we can know immediately by direct valid cognizers simply by seeing them, hearing them, smelling them, and so forth. Such objects are called 'manifest objects'. Other phenomena such as other people's minds of faith, intention and view are hidden objects for us. At present, we cannot gain a direct knowledge of these phenomena but, nevertheless, we can know them correctly with subsequent valid cognizers in dependence upon signs or reasons.

Likewise, emptiness is a hidden object and initially cannot be realized directly. First we must gain a correct understanding of the reasons that indicate emptiness and then subsequently, through contemplating these reasons, we can gain a subsequent valid realization of emptiness. Some books use the words 'inferential valid cognizer' instead of 'subsequent valid cognizer', but the meaning is the same.

Subsequent valid cognizers realizing emptiness are part of wisdom and can be of three types: wisdom arisen from listening, wisdom arisen from contemplation, and wisdom arisen from meditation. The first of these, wisdom arisen from listening, is a subsequent valid cognizer realizing emptiness that arises principally in dependence upon reasons that are explained by others. If we have very strong imprints from previous lives it is possible to realize emptiness without receiving instructions from others in this life, but generally we all need to listen to or read teachings on emptiness before we can gain a realization of it. Therefore, for most people, the mind that first realizes emptiness is wisdom arisen from listening. After having realized emptiness in this way, if we continue to contemplate and meditate, we can gain a more powerful realization of emptiness in dependence upon reasons established through our own contemplation. This is wisdom arisen from contemplation. Having developed this, if we continue to meditate on emptiness we gain a special valid experience of emptiness through the power of meditation. This special understanding is wisdom arisen from meditation. Although these three wisdoms all realize the same object, emptiness, there is a difference in their strength and how they arise. Wisdom arisen from meditation is more powerful than wisdom arisen from contemplation, which in turn is more powerful than wisdom arisen from listening.

Bodhisattvas on the path of accumulation improve their realization of emptiness principally by depending upon wisdom arisen from listening and wisdom arisen from contemplation. Bodhisattvas on this path have already attained tranquil abiding – a very supple, single-pointed concentration – since without tranquil abiding it is not possible to attain the perfect, non-fabricated mind of bodhichitta that is the gateway to the Mahayana paths. With their tranquil abiding concentration, they meditate on emptiness. Bodhisattvas on the path of accumulation are able to generate the wisdoms arisen from listening and from contemplation, but they are not able to generate the wisdom arisen from meditation observing emptiness. This last wisdom is the mind of superior seeing observing emptiness and is not possessed by Bodhisattvas on the path of accumulation.

Superior seeing observing emptiness develops out of the experience of meditating on emptiness with tranquil abiding. It is attained when the meditator attains a special suppleness induced by wisdom. The mind of superior seeing can investigate emptiness while at the same time remaining in single-pointed concentration on emptiness. Just as a small fish can swim in a still lake without disturbing the surface of the water, the mind of superior seeing can investigate emptiness without disturbing the concentration of tranquil abiding on emptiness.

The moment a Bodhisattva attains superior seeing observing emptiness, he or she has at that very moment attained the Mahayana path of preparation; and thus superior seeing observing emptiness is possessed by a Bodhisattva on the path of preparation but not by a Bodhisattva on the path of accumulation. Having attained the path of preparation, Bodhisattvas continue to enhance their practice of the perfection of wisdom by depending upon superior seeing observing emptiness – this being the wisdom arisen from meditation observing emptiness. Thus, although Bodhisattvas on both the paths of accumulation and preparation realize emptiness by means of subsequent valid cognizers, there are differences in the type of wisdom that observes emptiness on these two paths.

In summary, this part of Avalokiteshvara's answer explains that if we are a Mahayana practitioner wishing to develop the perfection of wisdom we should meditate on the emptiness of the person and of the five aggregates. While on the path of accumulation, we should enhance our understanding of emptiness by relying principally upon the wisdoms arisen from listening and contemplation. By strengthening our experience of emptiness, we will develop superior seeing observing emptiness and progress to the path of preparation. On this path, we should continue to meditate on emptiness by relying upon the wisdom arisen from meditation.

When we begin meditating on the emptiness of our self or any of our five aggregates – our body, feeling, discrimination, compositional factors and consciousness – with bodhichitta motivation, we are training in the perfection of wisdom.

AN EXTENSIVE EXPLANATION OF HOW TO TRAIN IN THE PERFECTION OF WISDOM ON THE PATHS OF ACCUMULATION AND PREPARATION

In the previous part of the Sutra, Avalokiteshvara gave a brief explanation of how to practise the perfection of wisdom while on the Mahayana paths of accumulation and preparation. The next part of his answer explains this practice in more detail, and is discussed under two outlines:

1 The explanation of the four profundities of the aggregate of form
2 The explanation of the four profundities of the aggregates of feeling and so forth

THE EXPLANATION OF THE FOUR PROFUNDITIES OF THE AGGREGATE OF FORM

Generally, there are four profundities:

(1) The profundity of the ultimate
(2) The profundity of the conventional
(3) The profundity of the two truths being the same entity
(4) The profundity of the two truths being nominally distinct

Avalokiteshvara first presents the four profundities of the aggregate of form. This part of his answer is therefore discussed under four outlines:

1 The explanation of the profundity of the ultimate of the aggregate of form
2 The explanation of the profundity of the conventional of the aggregate of form
3 The explanation of the profundity of the union of the two truths of the aggregate of form
4 The explanation of the profundity of the nominal distinction of the two truths of the aggregate of form

THE EXPLANATION OF THE PROFUNDITY OF THE ULTIMATE OF THE AGGREGATE OF FORM

Form is empty

The profundity of the ultimate of the aggregate of form is the emptiness of form, which means that form is empty of inherent existence. The emptiness of form is the ultimate nature of form, and because it is a very profound topic it is called 'the profundity of the ultimate of the aggregate of form'.

First we should identify what are the five aggregates. As mentioned before, the five aggregates are form, feeling, discrimination, compositional factors and consciousness. They are called 'aggregates' because they are each a composition of many elements.

Form includes all the objects of the five sense consciousnesses – everything that our eyes can see, our ears can hear, our nose can smell, our tongue can taste, and our body can sense or touch. All gross physical objects, such as mountains, tables and books, as well as all colours and shapes, sounds, smells, tastes and tactile objects are therefore included in the aggregate of form. The aggregate of form of a person is the person's body.

Feeling is a part of consciousness whose function is to experience happiness, unhappiness or indifference. It is a mental factor that accompanies all types of consciousness. When a primary mind comes into contact with its object, feeling functions to experience the object as pleasant, unpleasant or neutral. There are therefore three types of feeling: pleasant feelings, unpleasant feelings and neutral feelings.

Discrimination is a part of consciousness whose function is to recognize the uncommon signs or characteristics of an object. With discrimination we can distinguish one object from another, right from wrong, and so forth. Without feeling and discrimination our mind would be unable to function, and we would be unable to do anything.

Compositional factors comprise two types of phenomenon: mental factors and non-associated compounded phenomena. In total, there are fifty-one mental factors, and all except feeling and discrimination are included in the aggregate of compositional factors. This aggregate includes the other all-accompanying mental factors – attention, intention and contact; virtuous mental factors such as faith and effort; mental factors that are delusions such as anger and jealousy; and other types of mental factor such as mindfulness and regret. Non-associated compounded phenomena are all impermanent phenomena that are neither form nor mind, such as persons, life, time and potentialities. Persons are included in this category because they are impermanent, and although a person has a mind and has form, the phenomenon person itself is neither mind nor form. The aggregate of compositional factors of a person includes all the compositional factors within the continuum of the person.

Consciousness is a primary mind whose function is to cognize the general aspect of an object. The aggregate of consciousness includes the six primary minds, namely eye consciousness, ear consciousness, nose consciousness, tongue consciousness, body consciousness and mental consciousness.

We should know that our own five aggregates are our own body, feelings, discriminations, compositional factors and consciousness, and that these are the bases of imputation of our self. Through perceiving any of these five, because of ignorance we develop the thought 'I' or 'me'. But in fact, none of these five aggregates is our self.

In this Sutra, the aggregate of form is taken as the first basis for establishing emptiness. Also, in the *Perfection of Wisdom Sutra in One Hundred Thousand Lines*, in which one hundred and eight objects of knowledge from form to omniscience are taken as bases for establishing emptiness, form is taken as the first basis. Once we have realized emptiness using one basis, such as form, it is not difficult to establish the emptiness of other phenomena.

Emptiness is interpreted somewhat differently in the various Buddhist schools. The presentation given here is in accordance with the Madhyamika-Prasangika system of tenets, which is Buddha's ultimate view as expounded in the *Perfection of Wisdom Sutras*. Buddha taught different philosophical systems according to the various needs and capabilities of his followers, but his intention was to lead all living beings eventually to the final view of the Madhyamika-Prasangika school. There is no higher view than this.

Samantabhadra

According to the Madhyamika-Prasangika school, emptiness is the mere absence of inherent existence. Thus, when Avalokiteshvara says that form 'is empty', he means that form, such as our body, is empty of inherent existence, or that form does not exist inherently. To understand the significance of this, it is necessary to understand the meaning of inherent existence. We need to understand what would be the characteristics of an object if it existed inherently.

If something were inherently existent, it would have an existence within itself, independent of other phenomena. According to the Madhyamika-Prasangika school, if an object were inherently existent it would also be truly existent and existent from its own side. An object would be truly existent if it existed truly as it appeared and could be found upon investigation. Something would exist from its own side if its existence were established from the side of the object itself without depending upon an apprehending consciousness.

If we are ordinary beings, all objects appear to us to exist inherently. Objects seem to be independent of our mind and independent of other phenomena. The universe appears to consist of discrete objects that have an existence from their own side. These objects appear to exist in themselves as stars, planets, mountains, people and so forth, 'waiting' to be experienced by conscious beings. Normally it does not occur to us that we are involved in any way in the existence of these phenomena. Instead, each object appears to have an existence completely independent of us and all other objects.

With his words 'form is empty' Avalokiteshvara is saying that although objects that are included in the aggregate of form appear to exist inherently in this way, in reality they totally lack inherent existence. The way in which these objects actually exist is quite different from the way in which they appear to exist.

The question of whether objects exist inherently or not is extremely important because all our sufferings and dissatisfaction can be traced to our clinging to the inherent existence of ourself and other phenomena. It is necessary to realize that phenomena lack inherent existence in order to gain liberation from suffering and to attain full enlightenment.

As explained previously, until we attain the path of seeing, we need to rely upon logical reasons to realize emptiness. This Sutra does not explicitly explain the reasons that prove the emptiness of form, but many reasons are given in the longer *Perfection of Wisdom Sutras*. These reasons can be extracted and used here. The explanations of emptiness given in the *Perfection of Wisdom Sutra in One Hundred Thousand Lines* are condensed in the two shorter *Perfection of Wisdom Sutras* containing twenty-five thousand and eight thousand lines, and also in the *Condensed Perfection of Wisdom Sutra*. Although the explanations are condensed in the shorter Sutras, all the essential reasons given in the extensive Sutra are retained.

In the *Condensed Perfection of Wisdom Sutra*, Buddha says that form and the other aggregates are empty of inherent existence because, just as the depth of the ocean cannot be measured by shooting an arrow, if we investigate the aggregates with wisdom we cannot find them. It is clear that if we were to shoot an arrow into the ocean we could not discover the depth of the ocean in this way. Similarly, if we investigate the aggregates using sharp wisdom we will not find anything that we can point to and say, 'This is the aggregate of form', and so forth. If we are not content to accept the mere name 'aggregates' but instead try to discover the aggregates themselves we will be unable to find them. The fact that the aggregates cannot be found when investigated with wisdom is a reason used by Buddha to show that the aggregates lack inherent existence.

Our inability to find form upon analytical investigation can therefore be used to prove that form is empty. We can take our body as an example of the aggregate of form to illustrate how the reason may be applied. If we are ordinary beings, at present we have a view of our body as being inherently existent. Our body seems to be a single entity independent of the rest of the universe, and does not seem to rely on any conceptual process for its existence – it appears to us to be a solid, discrete object existing under its own power. Viewing our body in this way, we cherish it and react accordingly to cold, hunger, gentle caresses and so forth.

If our body really were inherently existent as it appears to be, we would expect to be able to find it upon investigation. This follows because our body would exist under its own power, independently of other phenomena, and therefore we could physically or mentally remove all objects that are not our body, and our body would still remain, existing by itself. Therefore, if we had an inherently existent body we should be able to point to our body without pointing to any phenomenon that is not our body.

We can check to see whether we can find our body in this way. If we wish to point to our body, what do we point to? We may point to the centre of our body, around our chest, or we may point to our head, arm, leg and so on. If, when we point to our chest, we are pointing to our body, it follows that our chest must be our body. If this is so, then equally our head must be our body, our arm must be our body, and so forth. It is clear that these objects are parts of our body, but they are not our body itself. If they were, it would follow that we had many bodies since there are many parts of the body. This is obviously nonsense. Alternatively, since we have only one body, if the parts of our body are our body itself it follows that the parts of our body are a single object. This also is nonsense. We must conclude that when we point to a part of our body such as our chest we are pointing to a phenomenon that is not our body itself. We can be sure, therefore, that upon investigation we cannot find our body among its individual parts.

As we continue to search for our body, we may think that the collection of the various parts of our body is our body. We may feel that when we point to the collection of our chest, head, arms and so forth, we have found our body. We need to investigate this possibility carefully. We have already established that each individual part of our body is not our body. The collection of the parts of our body is therefore a collection of objects that are not a body. We can say it is a collection of 'non-bodies'. It is impossible for a mere collection of non-bodies to be a body, just as it is impossible for a collection of non-sheep, for example goats, to be sheep. Since a collection of sheep is sheep and a collection of books is books, it follows that a collection of non-bodies is non-bodies and cannot possibly be a body. We can conclude, therefore, that the collection of parts of our body is parts of our body but not our body itself.

There is another way to know that the collection of the parts of our body is not our body. If we can point to the collection of the parts of our body and say that this, in itself, is our body, then the collection of the parts of our body must exist independently of all phenomena that are not our body, so it would follow that the collection of the parts of our body exists independently of the parts themselves. This is clearly absurd. If it were true we could remove all the parts of our body and the collection of the parts would remain. Again we can conclude that the collection of the parts of our body cannot be identified as our body itself.

So far we have been unable to find our body among the individual parts of our body or the collection of the parts of our body. The only remaining place to find our body is completely separate from the parts of our body. If our body existed in such a way, we could remove all the parts of our body and our body would still remain. Quite clearly this is not the case. We must conclude that we cannot find anything separate from the parts of our body that we can point to as our body.

We have now considered all possible places where we can find our body and have failed to locate it. If our body really did exist inherently as it appears to, we would be able to find it by isolating it from all other phenomena. Since we cannot succeed in doing this, we can come to the firm conclusion that our body that we normally see does not exist at all.

Unless we investigate in this way we naturally hold the view that we have a body that has its own independent existence. We feel that we can see and point to this self-existing body. However, in truth, whenever we see or point to our body, we are seeing or pointing to parts of our body, which are not our body. We should investigate this point carefully. When we say we see our body, what in fact do we see? We see only the parts of our body – our arms, legs and so forth. When we look at our body there is nothing that we see that is not a part of our body, and if something is a part of our body it is necessarily not our body. As already pointed out, if each part of our body were our body, it would follow that we have many bodies. We may propose that the collection of the parts of our body is our body, but the collection of the parts of our body is still just parts of our body. When we see the collection of the parts of our body we see only parts of our body.

If we apprehend a body that is other than the parts of the body, that apprehended body is what is called the 'inherently existent body'. This is the negated object of the emptiness of our body. However hard we search, we will never find such a body. When we look for our body we perceive only the parts of our body. Other than these parts there is no body to be found.

When we search for our body we are unable to find it. We may think that although we cannot find our body itself, at least we can find its parts – the head, the arms and so forth. However, if we investigate more carefully, taking our head as an example, we again experience difficulty in finding the object of our investigation. When we try to point to our head we point to our nose, eyes, cheek and so forth. The same arguments that were used to show that the parts of our body are not our body can be used to demonstrate that the parts of our head are not our head. Similarly, the collection of the parts of our head is not our head, nor can our head be found anywhere else. In this way we can realize that our head does not exist inherently. We can apply the same reasoning to demonstrate that our nose, the living cells of our nose, and even the molecules and atoms making up the cells are all empty, like space.

The emptiness of our body and its parts can be illustrated by considering the analogy of a toy snake. If someone places a toy rubber snake in our room, the first time we see it we may believe that it is a real snake and be quite startled by it. Even though there is no actual snake in our room, a snake appears vividly to our mind. For a short time, we may cling to this appearance as real and develop fear as a result. However, if we look more carefully we will discover that the snake does not exist in the way that it appears. Clearly there is no real snake existing from its own side; we have merely imputed a snake with our conceptual mind. Apart from the mere appearance of a snake to our mind, there is no real snake to be found anywhere in our room. When we realize this, all our fears associated with the snake immediately subside.

If we check carefully, we discover that our body and the snake that appears to our mind in the above analogy exist in a very similar way. Just like the snake, our body appears vividly to our mind and seems to exist from its own side. However, as with the snake, if we investigate we are unable to find our body and we discover that it has no existence of its own but is merely imputed by our mind. Like the snake, our body is a mere appearance to our mind. As long as we believe that it has its own inherent existence our body can be a source of fear and pain, but when we realize that it is merely imputed by our mind these fears and so forth will decrease and eventually disappear, just as our fear of the snake is overcome when we realize that it is only imputed.

Although the snake and our body exist in a very similar way, there is an important difference. When we discover that the snake is really a toy snake and realize that the real snake was merely imputed by our mind, we conclude that a real snake does not exist at all in our room. However, when we realize that our body is merely imputed by our mind, according to the common view it would be a great mistake to conclude that our body does not exist at all. It is true that the inherently existent body that normally appears to our mind has no more existence than the real snake that appears to be in our room – both are completely

non-existent – but a body that is empty of inherent existence and is merely imputed upon the collection of the
parts of our body does exist. A merely imputed body exists
because the parts of our body are, by convention, a suitable
basis on which to impute a body because they can perform
the functions of a body. A length of striped rubber, on the
other hand, is not a suitable basis on which to impute a real
snake because it cannot perform the functions of a snake.
Therefore, in the analogy described above, we say that a
real snake does not exist at all in our room. Both the snake
and our body are merely imputed by our mind, but our
body is imputed correctly whereas the snake is imputed
incorrectly. To overcome the sufferings associated with
our body, we need to understand that the body that we
normally see, the inherently existent body, does not exist;
but to perform our daily activities, we need to accept that
the merely imputed body does exist.

Another analogy that is often used to illustrate the meaning of emptiness is the experience of dreaming. When we
dream we may have extremely vivid experiences. We may
travel to colourful lands, meet beautiful or terrifying people,
engage in various activities, and as a result experience great
pleasure or suffering and pain. In our dream a whole world
appears to us, functioning in its own way. This world may
be similar to the world of our waking state or it may be quite
bizarre, but in either case while we are dreaming it appears
to be utterly real. It is quite rare to have even the slightest
suspicion that what we are experiencing is just a dream. The
world we inhabit in our dream seems to have its own existence completely independent of our mind, and we respond
to that world in our normal way, with desire, anger, fear and
so on.

If while we are still dreaming we try to test whether the world we are experiencing is real or not, for example by tapping the objects around us or by questioning the other people in our dream, we will probably get a response that seems to confirm the reality of our dream surroundings. In fact, the only way to know for certain that we have been dreaming is to wake up. Then we immediately realize without any doubt that the world we were experiencing in our dream was deceptive and was merely an appearance to our mind. It is quite clear once we are awake that what we experienced in a dream does not exist from its own side but depends completely upon our mind. For example, if we dream of an elephant, the 'dream elephant' is merely an appearance to our mind and cannot be found inside our bedroom or elsewhere.

If we check carefully we will realize that the way our waking world exists is similar to the way our dream world exists. Like the dream world, our waking world appears vividly to us and seems to have its own existence independent of our mind; and just as in a dream we believe this appearance to be true, and respond with desire, anger, fear and so on. Also, if we superficially test our waking world as we did our dream world to see whether it really does exist in the way that it appears, we will again receive an apparent confirmation of our view. If we tap the objects around us they will appear to be quite solid and real, and if we ask other people, they will say they see the same objects in the same way as we do. However, we should not take this apparent confirmation of the inherent existence of objects as conclusive because we know that similar tests cannot reveal the actual nature of our dream world. To understand the true nature of our waking world we must investigate and meditate deeply, using the type of analysis already described. When by these means we realize emptiness we will understand that objects such as our body do not exist from their own side. Like the dream elephant, they are mere appearances to our mind. Nevertheless our world functions, following its own apparent rules in accordance with the laws of cause and effect, just as our dream world functions in its own way.

The experience of realizing emptiness can therefore be compared to waking up. Once we realize emptiness we see clearly and without any doubt that the world as we experienced it before was deceptive and false. It appeared to have its own inherent existence, but, having understood emptiness, we realize that it is completely empty of inherent existence and depends upon our mind. In fact, Buddha is sometimes called the 'Awakened One' because he has awakened from the 'sleep' of ignorance.

In Buddha's scriptures, emptiness is often compared to space. We say that we see space, but we do not normally check what kind of space we are seeing; we are satisfied with just the name 'space'. If we investigate to find out what we are actually seeing when we say we see space, we will not be able to find anything – it is just empty. Similarly, if we are not satisfied with the mere name 'my body' but try to find out what kind of body we see, we will discover that we cannot see our body at all. Our body is also empty, like space.

Although we talk about empty space, the empty space we normally refer to is not the same as the emptiness of our body. However, empty space is the best analogy to help us to understand the meaning of profound emptiness, so we need to understand clearly the meaning of space.

There are two types of space: produced space and unproduced space. Produced space is the visible space that we can see inside a room or in the sky. This space may become

dark at night and light during the day, and because it under-
goes change in this way it is an impermanent phenomenon
and can be seen with our eyes. The characteristic property
of produced space is that it does not obstruct objects. For
example, if there is space in a room we can place objects there
without obstruction. Similarly birds are able to fly through
the space of the sky because it lacks obstruction, whereas
they cannot fly through a mountain! Therefore, we can say
that produced space lacks, or is empty of, obstructive contact.
This mere lack of obstructive contact is unproduced space.
Since unproduced space is the mere absence of obstructive
contact it does not undergo momentary change and is therefore a permanent phenomenon. Whereas produced space is
visible and quite easy to know, unproduced space is a mere
absence and is rather more subtle. However, once we understand unproduced space we will find it easier to understand
emptiness.

Unproduced space is a negative phenomenon. A negative
phenomenon is a phenomenon that is realized through the
explicit elimination of the phenomenon's object of negation
by the mind that apprehends that phenomenon. In the case of
unproduced space, the object of negation is obstructive contact, and space is realized by a mind that explicitly eliminates
this object of negation. Furthermore, unproduced space is a
non-affirming negative, which means that unproduced space
is realized by a mind through its elimination of the object of
negation without that mind realizing another positive object.
The mind that realizes unproduced space negates obstructive
contact but does not affirm any other phenomenon. In contrast, some phenomena are affirming negatives. An affirming
negative is a phenomenon that is realized by a mind that
explicitly eliminates the phenomenon's object of negation

and that indirectly realizes a positive phenomenon. An example of an affirming negative is my cousin's lack of being female, since the mind that realizes my cousin's lack of being female indirectly realizes that my cousin is male. On the other hand, unproduced space does not imply any positive phenomenon – it is the mere absence of obstructive contact.

Like unproduced space, all emptinesses are non-affirming negatives. For example, the emptiness of our body is the mere lack, or absence, of our body that we normally see, the inherently existent body – no other object is implied. Thus, the mind that realizes the emptiness of our body merely eliminates the object of negation without realizing any positive phenomenon. The non-affirming negative that is the mere absence of our body that we normally see is the emptiness of our body.

Both unproduced space and emptiness are non-affirming negatives but they have different objects of negation. The negated object of unproduced space is obstructive contact, whereas the negated object of emptiness is inherent existence. It is because unproduced space and emptiness differ only in their objects of negation that an understanding of unproduced space is so helpful in gaining an understanding of emptiness.

To understand unproduced space we must first know its negated object, obstructive contact. This is not very difficult to know – even insects appear to know what it is. For example, an insect will walk across a table as long as it can sense the obstructive contact of the table's surface, but will turn back when it reaches the edge of the table where the obstructive contact ceases. It seems that the insect knows what obstructive contact is and so can recognize its absence. If we understand what is meant by obstructive contact and know that unproduced space is simply the mere absence of this, we are then able to realize the meaning of unproduced space. Similarly, if we wish to realize emptiness we must first understand the negated object of emptiness, inherent existence. For example, in the case of the emptiness of the body, the negated object is the inherently existing body – the body that we normally see. Therefore, to understand the emptiness of the body we must first be familiar with the appearance and characteristics of an inherently existent body so that we are clear what object is negated by the mind realizing emptiness. 'Inherently existent things', 'truly existent things' and 'things that we normally see' are synonymous, and they are all the negated object of emptiness. We need to know that they do not exist at all.

An inherently existent body would be a body that is independent of other phenomena, including the mind apprehending it. If we check carefully we will discover that our body appears to us to exist in this way at present. In fact, whatever appears to the mind of an ordinary being necessarily appears to be inherently existent, and for this reason all the minds of ordinary beings are mistaken. Until we realize emptiness we cling very strongly to our body with the thought, 'my body, my body', and the body that appears vividly to our mind at that time is an inherently existent body. Our mistaken mind believes that this body really exists, and as a result we cling to it and develop strong attachment towards it. We then cherish this body, worry about it, and do many actions for its sake. In fact, this body does not exist at all. Thus, the body that we normally perceive and cling to as 'my body' is the actual negated object of the emptiness of our body. The body that we normally perceive and cling to does not exist. It is important to realize this.

Although there does not exist anywhere an inherently existent body, the generic image of an inherently existent body does exist. A generic image is the mental image of an object that appears to our conceptual mind whenever we think about that object. For example, if we think about our mother, a characteristic image of our mother appears vividly to our mind. This appearing image is the generic image of our mother. However, an object need not exist for its generic image to appear to us. For example, the generic image of a unicorn can appear vividly to our mind, but although this generic image exists a unicorn itself does not. Similarly, whenever we think about our body the generic image of an inherently existent body appears to our conceptual mind, but it is an image of something that is totally non-existent. Nevertheless, before we can correctly realize the emptiness of our body we must identify precisely this inherently existent body, which is the object of negation. Therefore, in meditation we need to become thoroughly familiar with the generic image of this body as it appears to us.

Buddhist philosophical treatises explain that the negated object of emptiness is inherent existence. However, if we think that we are negating inherent existence but fail to negate the body that we normally see, we have not found the correct object of negation. The correct object of negation is precisely the body that we normally see. Therefore, if we say that we are negating inherent existence but do not negate the body that normally appears to us, we are merely negating inherent existence 'with our mouth'.

When it is said that the body that normally appears vividly to us does not exist, some people may misunderstand this and think that the existence of phenomena is being denied completely. It is therefore very important to think deeply and with sharp wisdom about this matter. We need to identify precisely the negated object of emptiness. If the object we negate is too extensive we will negate something that actually exists, and thereby fall into the extreme of non-existence. This would be the case if we were to deny that our body exists at all. On the other hand, if the object we negate is too limited we will continue to accept a degree of inherent existence and thereby fall into the extreme of existence. For example, if we negate a body that is independent of its parts but posit a body that possesses its own inherent nature there still remains an object to be negated and we have fallen into the extreme of existence.

The correct view of emptiness avoids both extremes and therefore emptiness is called the 'middle way'. The extreme of non-existence is avoided because the correct view of emptiness accepts the existence of phenomena that are merely imputed in dependence upon a valid basis of imputation, and the extreme of existence is avoided because the correct view of emptiness thoroughly negates all traces of inherent, independent existence.

If we wish to understand emptiness clearly without any mistake and already have a basic understanding of Buddhist teachings, then on this basis it is very important to practise purification and accumulate merit. Having prepared our mind in this way, if we then study and meditate on emptiness continually there is great hope that we will attain a correct realization of emptiness.

Although we need to strive to develop a new realization of emptiness, it is important to understand that emptiness itself is not a new development or creation. It is not a product of philosophical analysis or an invention of Buddha. Emptiness has been the actual nature of all phenomena from the very beginning. Our body, for example, has always been empty of inherent existence; there has never been a time when our body, or anything else, existed inherently. Although emptiness has always been the true nature of phenomena, we need to receive instructions to realize this; and for this reason Buddha taught the *Perfection of Wisdom Sutras*.

It is important to strive to understand the emptiness of phenomena because all the problems and suffering we and other living beings experience stem from a mistaken view of reality. Through our ignorance of the true nature of phenomena, we develop the conceptual mind that holds phenomena to be inherently existent. This mind is known as 'self-grasping' because it apprehends, or grasps, phenomena as having an inherently existent self, or identity. The mind of self-grasping gives rise to all other delusions such as anger and attachment, and is the root cause of all suffering and dissatisfaction. Therefore, if we wish to be free from suffering we must abandon our self-grasping.

To realize emptiness and overcome our self-grasping, we must first receive correct instructions and then meditate on how our body and other phenomena are empty of inherent existence. First we should do analytical meditation by investigating with our wisdom whether we can find our body. Is this body that we cherish as 'my body' the same as the parts of our body? Are our head, arms and so forth our body? Can we find a body that is different from the parts of our body? Through this investigation we will discover that our body is unfindable. If our analytical meditation is successful, the appearance of our body will fade and there will arise an appearance of 'empty'. This emptiness is our body's emptiness. We should try to hold the generic image of this emptiness single-pointedly in placement meditation.

If we begin to lose the generic image of emptiness we should recall the reasons used to establish our body's emptiness and thereby restore our object of meditation. Through this meditation we can become familiar with emptiness and strengthen our realization.

In the beginning during our meditations on emptiness we should not worry about falling into the extreme of non-existence because during meditation we are not performing actions of body and speech. It is when we are out of meditation and performing various actions that we need to be careful to avoid this extreme. However, if we identify correctly the negated object of emptiness there is no danger of developing extreme views. We need to know that our body does not exist inherently but does exist conventionally. The conventional nature of our body is explained in the next chapter.

If during our meditation on emptiness we develop any doubts or see any contradictions, we should discuss these afterwards with a skilled Teacher or experienced friends. In Tibet, when a Lama gave instructions on emptiness and so forth, the students would listen and then meditate on the teachings for a few days. They would then describe their experiences to the Lama and discuss any problems they were having. In this way, all doubts were clarified and the students then returned to their meditation. That is the way we should try to realize emptiness. If we develop doubts or cannot accept what is taught we should discuss the matter with others. In this way, our understanding will become clearer and clearer. We should not keep doubts hidden inside our hearts – we need wisdom in our hearts, not doubts!

Through receiving instructions and then contemplating and meditating on the meaning we can realize that our body and other forms are unfindable upon investigation. This unfindability is our body's emptiness. It indicates that our body does not exist objectively, from its own side. Our body is only a mere apprehension of the mind, a mere appearance to the mind. Perceiving this appearance we say 'my body', but if we are not satisfied with the mere name 'my body' and try to find a body existing from its own side we will be completely unsuccessful. Through meditating on the emptiness of our body as described, our delusions such as attachment towards our body will be subdued. Similarly, if we have problems of strong attachment towards the bodies of others we should think, 'Just as my body that I normally see does not exist, so too the bodies of others that I normally see do not exist.' Thinking in this way we meditate on the mere absence of the bodies of others that we normally see. In this way our attachment will be reduced.

Through improving our understanding of emptiness we can build the foundation for attaining ultimate happiness. Whether we are rich or poor, beautiful or ugly, we can solve all our problems and fulfil all our wishes through the wisdom that realizes emptiness. By doing continual meditation on emptiness we will gradually gain freedom from all suffering by uprooting its cause, ignorance. Then even if we wish for suffering we will be unable to experience it! If we gain the wisdom realizing emptiness we will be like a king and our wisdom realizing emptiness will be like the king's ministers. Just as all the king's wishes are accomplished by his ministers, so too will all our wishes be accomplished by our wisdom realizing emptiness.

Although our body has been taken as the basis for establishing emptiness, all other forms, and indeed all phenomena, are empty of inherent existence in the same way. To realize that all phenomena are empty of inherent existence we do not need to realize the emptiness of each phenomenon one by one. If we understand emptiness correctly using one basis such as our body we can, without difficulty, realize the emptiness of all other phenomena by changing the basis of emptiness.

In summary, Avalokiteshvara's words 'form is empty' teach that all form is empty of inherent existence – this emptiness being the profundity of the ultimate of form. Without realizing this profundity we cannot gain either complete freedom from suffering or full enlightenment. Thus, Avalokiteshvara indicates that the principal practice of the perfection of wisdom while on the Mahayana paths of accumulation and preparation is meditation on emptiness. On these two paths, we need to realize emptiness with a generic image using the type of reasoning described in this chapter.

Ksitigarbha

The Paths of Accumulation and Preparation (2)

The previous chapter explained the profundity of the ultimate of form as stated in the Sutra by the words 'form is empty'. This presentation revealed the ultimate nature of form. The next part of Avalokiteshvara's answer presents the three remaining profundities of form and thereby reveals form's subtle conventional nature.

THE EXPLANATION OF THE PROFUNDITY OF THE CONVENTIONAL OF THE AGGREGATE OF FORM

Emptiness is form

Whereas the profundity of the ultimate of a phenomenon is the phenomenon's emptiness, the profundity of the conventional is the phenomenon's being a manifestation of emptiness.

Although the second, third and fourth profundities are all part of the conventional nature of phenomena, they are called 'profundities' because they are the subtle conventional nature of phenomena, which is even more difficult to realize than phenomena's ultimate nature. Furthermore, we cannot gain a perfect and complete understanding of profound emptiness until we have understood the subtle conventional nature of phenomena.

To understand what is meant by the ultimate and conventional natures of phenomena we need to understand what is meant by the two truths – ultimate truths and conventional truths. The two truths are actual objects, or phenomena, and not just abstract philosophical laws or principles. In fact, every phenomenon that exists is either an ultimate truth or a conventional truth, but no phenomenon can be both.

'Ultimate truth' and 'emptiness' are synonyms – whatever is an ultimate truth is an emptiness and whatever is an emptiness is an ultimate truth. The emptiness of our body and the emptiness of this book are examples of ultimate truths. All ultimate truths are the same in that they are emptinesses, but they differ in the basis of emptiness, the object that is empty.

An emptiness is called an 'ultimate truth' (Tib. don dam denpa), literally a 'sacred object truth', because emptiness is both a sacred object and a truth. It is a sacred object because the realization of emptiness opens the door of liberation. We may realize many other phenomena but if we do not realize emptiness we will be unable to gain liberation. An emptiness is a truth because its appearance to a non-conceptual direct perceiver is in accordance with its mode of existence. To a mind realizing an emptiness directly, only emptiness appears; inherent existence does not appear at all. Thus, when cognized directly, an emptiness does not falsely appear to be inherently existent. Because its appearance does not deceive us an emptiness is a truth.

All phenomena except emptinesses are conventional truths. For example, our body and this book are two conventional truths. Unlike ultimate truths, which are all emptinesses, conventional truths are extremely diverse since they include every object of knowledge that is not an emptiness. Conventional truths are not actually truths in the way that ultimate truths are, because their apparent mode of existence does not accord with their actual mode of existence – conventional truths appear to be inherently existent but in reality they are empty of inherent existence. Since their appearance is deceptive, conventional truths are in fact falsities, not truths. However, they are called 'conventional truths' because they are true with respect to the conventions of ordinary people, that is, people who have not realized emptiness directly. Conventional truths are true with respect to the view of ordinary people because although conventional truths are deceptive regarding their mode of existence they are not deceptive regarding their function and conventional characteristics. For example, a table that is apprehended by a valid mind is a conventional truth, and we can rely upon such a table to support objects and perform the other functions of a table. Objects that are false with respect to the minds of ordinary people, such as a table seen by someone who is hallucinating, are not conventional truths. They are non-existents and cannot be relied upon to perform the functions they appear to possess.

The term that has been translated as conventional truth (Tib. kun dzob denpa) can also be rendered as 'truth for an obscurer'. Here, 'obscurer' refers to self-grasping – the mind that conceives phenomena to be inherently existent. Phenomena other than ultimate truths are called 'truths for an obscurer' because with respect to the mind of self-grasping they are true; they appear to be inherently existent and the mind of self-grasping holds this appearance to be true.

However, it does not follow that the mind of self-grasping apprehends and establishes conventional truths. The object held by self-grasping is an inherently existent object, such as an inherently existent body, and, as already explained, there does not exist an inherently existent object anywhere. The object held by self-grasping is therefore a non-existent and consequently not a conventional truth. Like ultimate truths, conventional truths are established by a valid mind, and self-grasping is not a valid mind. Thus, a conventional object is called a 'truth for an obscurer' not because the object is established by the mind of self-grasping but because self-grasping ignorantly conceives the apparent inherent existence of the object to be true.

As we can understand from the above, it is important to distinguish between conventional truths and non-existents. A traditional example of a non-existent is a horn on the head of a rabbit. Although the ears of a rabbit can appear to be a horn and we can conceive of a rabbit having a horn, we know that this appearance is mistaken and the conception is false. A horn on a rabbit's head is not established by any valid mind and consequently is a non-existent, not a conventional (or ultimate) truth. In the same way, although inherently exist-ent objects appear to the mind and are objects of conception, they are totally non-existent and therefore not conventional truths.

Thus, when it is said that a table is a conventional truth, the meaning is that the table that is apprehended by a valid mind is a conventional truth; it does not mean that the inherently existent table that appears to the minds of ordinary beings is a conventional truth. For example, if we perceive a table with a valid eye consciousness, unless we are a fully enlightened being the table will appear to be inherently existent to our eye consciousness. However, our eye consciousness does not apprehend the table to be inherently existent; it apprehends simply the table itself. The table that is correctly apprehended by our eye consciousness in this way is a conventional truth and does exist (but not inherently). It is probable that following the valid eye consciousness that apprehends just the table itself we will develop a conceptual mental consciousness that apprehends the table as inherently existent. This conceptual mind is a mind of self-grasping. It is a non-valid mind and the object it grasps is a non-existent.

We can now consider what is meant by the ultimate nature and conventional nature of phenomena. The ultimate nature of a phenomenon is the phenomenon's emptiness, and because it is an emptiness it is an ultimate truth. The conventional nature of a phenomenon is the phenomenon's nature as established by a valid mind, but excluding emptiness. Since the conventional nature is established by a valid mind it is an existent, and since it is an existent and not an emptiness it is a conventional truth. We can consider a table as an example to illustrate the meaning of these two natures. The table's emptiness is the table's ultimate nature; the table itself and its shape, colour and so forth are all the conventional nature of the table. Any phenomenon such as a table has an ultimate nature and a conventional nature. The former is an ultimate truth and the latter is a conventional truth.

The conventional nature of an object can have many aspects. Some of these aspects, such as an object's shape and colour, can be realized simply by direct sense awareness, whereas others, such as an object's impermanence, are more difficult to realize. Some aspects of the conventional nature of an object can be realized only after having realized the object's ultimate nature. That part of the conventional nature of an object that cannot be realized without first realizing the object's ultimate nature is the subtle conventional nature of the object.

As already stated, the profundity of the conventional – the second of the four profundities – is phenomena being manifestations of emptiness, and is part of phenomena's subtle conventional nature. It is part of the conventional nature rather than the ultimate nature because it is not an emptiness and is therefore a conventional truth rather than an ultimate truth. It is part of the subtle conventional nature of phenomena because we cannot realize that phenomena are manifestations of emptiness before we realize that phenomena are empty of inherent existence.

There are many scriptural references to phenomena as manifestations of emptiness. For example, in *Song of Emptiness* Changkya Rolpai Dorje says:

These various apprehended [objects] and apprehenders are manifestations of the mother. This birth, death, and these changing [things] are falsities of the mother.

Here, 'mother' refers to emptiness and 'falsities' to the false appearance of conventional truths.

When Avalokiteshvara says, 'emptiness is form', he is declaring the second profundity of form – that form is a manifestation of emptiness. What does it mean to say that form is a manifestation of emptiness? If we take our body as an example, the ultimate nature of our body is the emptiness of our body. If we search for our body there is no body. Nevertheless, from its emptiness a body, which is the nature of an empty like space, appears to our mind.

We can say therefore that our body is a manifestation of its emptiness.

This can be illustrated by taking the analogy of a gold coin. The underlying nature of the coin is gold; it is the gold itself that appears to us in the form of a coin. Clearly, the coin that appears to us is not different from its gold and there is no coin other than its gold. We can say therefore that the coin is a manifestation of its gold. In this analogy, the gold represents the emptiness of our body and the coin represents our body itself. Just as the coin is a manifestation of its gold, our body is a manifestation of its emptiness.

We can consider a rather more subtle illustration of the relationship between our body and its emptiness. A sky that is completely clear appears to us as blue. We know that the actual nature of the sky is merely empty, just as the space around us is empty. Although the sky appears to be a blue canopy, if we travel towards it we will never encounter a blue object; there is only space. Nevertheless, when we look at the sky we see blue and we point to this blue as being the sky. We can say therefore that the blue we see directly is a manifestation of an empty sky. Thus, from an empty sky, blue manifests. Similarly, from the emptiness of form, form manifests. In the same way, all phenomena are manifestations of their emptiness.

Another way to understand the profundity of the conventional is to realize that phenomena are mere appearances. The use of the word 'mere' eliminates any possibility of inherent existence. As explained previously, our body does not exist within its parts, yet there is no body other than its parts. How, then, does our body exist? It exists as a mere appearance to the mind. If we are satisfied with the mere appearance we can say, 'My body is healthy or unhealthy', and so forth. If we are not satisfied with the mere appearance and we search for our body we will discover that our body does not exist at all. This clearly proves that our body exists as a mere appearance to the mind. Our body existing as a mere appearance to mind is a very profound conventional phenomenon. All other phenomena exist in the same way.

To illustrate how our body is a mere appearance, we can consider the analogy of a rainbow. In certain conditions a rainbow appears in the sky. To the observer it appears that the rainbow has a certain size, shape and location in space. It seems to have its own existence, perhaps three or four miles away. However, we know that if we travel to the apparent location of the rainbow there will be no trace of a rainbow there. We can say therefore that the rainbow is a mere appearance and cannot be found upon investigation. Although other objects, such as our body, seem to have a more concrete existence, if we investigate carefully we will discover that they too are a mere appearance.

Through our experience, we know that the appearance of a rainbow is deceptive. It appears to have its own independent existence but we know that its existence depends on the sun, the rain and the position of the observer. If the observer moves, the rainbow moves; if the sun goes behind a cloud, the rainbow fades or disappears. Provided we accept that the rainbow is only an appearance that arises in dependence upon certain causes and conditions, we can accept its existence and behave appropriately. However, if we cling to the idea that the rainbow exists independently of us and is fixed in space in the way that it appears, we may travel in search of the 'end of the rainbow' and experience only frustration.

The same is true of all forms and of phenomena in general. If we accept them as mere appearances we can establish their existence and relate to them appropriately, without experiencing any problems. Again, though, if we cling to phenomena as existing inherently in the way that they appear we will experience constant problems and frustration. Just as through experience we have learnt the real nature of a rainbow, so through study and contemplation we can understand the subtle conventional nature of form and other phenomena, and begin to relate to them appropriately.

Another aspect of the subtle conventional nature of phenomena is that phenomena are mere name. We can imagine a committee consisting of a number of members, one of whom is called John. Let us suppose that today John is elected to be the Chairperson of the committee. From today, John will be called the 'Chairperson' and the other committee members will think of him as the Chairperson. The John of yesterday was not the Chairperson, whereas the John of today is, but from John's side there has been no particular change. John is now the Chairperson simply because he was so named by the committee. If we try to find something that from its own side is inherently a chairperson we will not succeed. John's body is not a chairperson, his mind is not a chairperson, and we will not find anything else that is a chairperson. In this example, it is not difficult to understand that 'Chairperson' is no more than name. In fact, if we investigate carefully we will discover that all phenomena exist in this way as mere name. Indeed, in the *Perfection of Wisdom Sutra in One Hundred Thousand Lines* Buddha says, 'Shariputra, know that all phenomena are mere name.'

Understanding that form is a mere appearance and mere name helps us to understand that form is a manifestation of emptiness. If we realize this, we can establish the existence of form without implying that form exists inherently. We can then begin to understand the subtle conventional nature of form and be able to avoid the two extremes of existence and non-existence.

The way in which the Madhyamika-Prasangikas establish the existence of conventional phenomena is actually in accordance with the view of ordinary people. In establishing the existence of a table, for example, ordinary people are content with the appearance of a table and the name 'table'. They do not normally carry out an investigation to find the real table. In a similar way, Madhyamika-Prasangikas say that phenomena are merely an appearance to our mind and mere name. They assert that if we try to find a real table apart from the mere appearance and the mere name we will not succeed.

In contrast to ordinary people and the Madhyamika-Prasangikas, other philosophical systems, including the lower Buddhist schools, assert that through investigation we can discover the real object. For example, when they search for the table among its parts, some Buddhist schools conclude that the mere collection of the parts of the table is the table. They say that this collection is the real, truly existent table. According to the Madhyamika-Prasangikas, this view contradicts the view of ordinary people because the table established in this way is not the table apprehended by ordinary people; it is merely a fabrication of philosophical analysis. The Madhyamika-Prasangikas say that there is no such thing as a truly existent phenomenon and so the table that the lower schools try to establish is in fact non-existent. For this reason, Chandrakirti warned the lower schools not to debate with ordinary people, for if they did so they would lose!

Although the Madhyamika-Prasangikas establish the existence of conventional phenomena in accordance with the view of ordinary people, their view of the ultimate nature of phenomena contradicts the view of ordinary people. Ordinary people not only accept the existence of objects that appear to them but they also accept objects as being inherently existent in the way that they appear. The Madhyamika-Prasangika view is that all objects are empty of inherent existence, and therefore, although the existence of conventional objects is to be accepted, if we wish to attain liberation we must abandon the mind that grasps at inherent existence. Furthermore, if we wish to attain full enlightenment, we must abandon even the appearance of objects as inherently existent.

Once we realize that phenomena are empty of inherent existence we can begin to understand their subtle conventional nature by meditating on them as manifestations of emptiness using some of the reasons and analogies given in this chapter. We can then carry the practice of seeing phenomena as manifestations of emptiness into our daily activities. Although we ordinary beings cannot meditate on emptiness while we are eating, working, talking and so forth, we can nevertheless see the objects around us as manifestations of emptiness. If we do this, our food, our body, our friends and so forth will still appear to be inherently existent but we will not accept this appearance. We can continue to perform our daily activities, yet at the same time remember that the things that we normally see do not exist. In this way, our wisdom realizing emptiness will increase continually. If we see everything as manifestations of emptiness our mind will naturally be free from delusions and our actions will be virtuous. Through this practice, our everyday activities can become extremely meaningful.

Emptiness is a permanent phenomenon, but manifestations of emptiness need not be permanent. Functioning things such as our body are impermanent, momentary phenomena, being the results of past causes and the causes of future effects, but they are all manifestations of emptiness. Our body functions and changes moment by moment but it does not exist from its own side; it is merely imputed by thought. Our body remains empty of inherent existence at all times, and out of this permanent emptiness our body appears to us in its constantly changing form.

With respect to the minds of Superior beings, conventional truths such as our body are false. However, with respect to the minds of ordinary beings, conventional truths are true because the mind of self-grasping of these beings holds the apparent inherent existence of conventional truths to be true. We need to understand that the forms and so forth that appear to us are manifestations of their emptiness and are mere name, but that they function and appear true to ordinary beings. Therefore, when performing our everyday activities, we should be satisfied with the mere name of phenomena without investigating them further. At that time there is no point in trying to discover a truly existent phenomenon because no such phenomenon can be found.

If, having realized emptiness, we are able to accept phenomena as mere name and engage in our various activities on this basis, this indicates that we have realized the subtle conventional nature of phenomena. Then we can still say that a particular object is large or small, for example, but we know that the object is mere name and cannot be found upon analysis.

If we have this correct understanding of the subtle conventional nature of phenomena we can understand that phenomena are empty of inherent existence but also perform their individual functions. In this way, the conventional nature of phenomena and their emptiness are seen not as contradictory but as mutually supportive. For example, realizing the emptiness of our body helps us to understand the conventional nature of our body as mere name or mere appearance, and realizing that our body is mere name helps us to understand that our body is empty of inherent existence. We need to strive to realize the two truths in this way.

THE EXPLANATION OF THE PROFUNDITY OF THE UNION OF THE TWO TRUTHS OF THE AGGREGATE OF FORM

Emptiness is not other than form; form also is not other than emptiness.

The meaning of these words is that the emptiness of form and form itself are not different objects but are the same entity. This same entity is called the 'union of the two truths of form', and is a very profound and subtle object. If we meditate on the emptiness of form with deep knowledge of the union of the two truths of form our meditation will have great power to eliminate our delusions quickly.

Conventional truths, such as our body, are just creations of our self-grasping ignorance that strongly thinks, 'my body, my body'. The question may then arise: 'How do conventional truths actually exist if they are just creations of the wrong awareness, self-grasping?' The correct answer to this question is very subtle.

Sarvanivaranaviskambini

As mentioned above, we can say that conventional truths actually exist, but this is only according to common appearance, the appearance of ordinary beings. According to the uncommon appearance of Superior beings who are meditating on emptiness there are no conventional truths because for them the appearance of conventional truths has been dispelled by dissolving their minds into emptiness completely. As Chandrakirti says in his *Guide to the Middle Way*, something that is created as truth by self-grasping ignorance is a conventional truth. This means that all conventional truths are just creations of self-grasping ignorance. This implies that the things that we normally perceive are also just creations of self-grasping ignorance.

This part of the Sutra reveals the union of the two truths, which is a very profound topic. 'Union' means 'that two things are one'. For example, for ordinary beings the body, which is a conventional truth, and the emptiness of the body, which is an ultimate truth, are two different things because they perceive them in this way. However, for enlightened beings these two truths are one in ultimate truth. In the state of enlightenment there are no conventional truths because conventional truths are mere creations of self-grasping, and enlightened beings do not have self-grasping ignorance.

THE EXPLANATION OF THE PROFUNDITY OF THE NOMINAL DISTINCTION OF THE TWO TRUTHS OF THE AGGREGATE OF FORM

The profundity of the nominal distinction of the two truths of the aggregate of form means that although form, which is a conventional truth, and the emptiness of form, which is an ultimate truth, are not two different things but one entity, we can distinguish them in dependence upon their mere name. This is also a very profound topic. If we understand clearly the distinction between the two truths of the aggregate of form while accepting that they are the same entity, we understand the profundity of the nominal distinction of the two truths of the aggregate of form. Through knowing this we will remain in the middle way (Tib. uma), free from the extremes of existence and non-existence. We can distinguish between the two truths of form by being completely satisfied with their mere names. By doing this, we will be free from both these extreme views.

In conclusion, Avalokiteshvara's answer to Shariputra's question reveals the four profundities of the aggregate of form – the profundity of the ultimate, the profundity of the conventional, the profundity of the union of the two truths, and the profundity of the nominal distinction of the two truths. The purpose of contemplating the explanation of the first profundity is to understand correctly the emptiness of form. The purpose of contemplating the explanation of the second profundity is to complete our understanding of the emptiness of form. The purpose of contemplating the explanation of the third profundity is to strengthen our understanding of the emptiness of form so that we are able to eliminate delusions quickly, and the purpose of contemplating the explanation of the fourth profundity is to free ourself completely from the extremes of existence and non-existence.

Having understood the emptiness of our body correctly, we meditate on this emptiness continually until we gain a deep experience of this meditation. We should also apply effort to understanding the subtle conventional truth of our body, that our body exists as mere name. When we succeed in this, our understanding of the emptiness of our body is complete. Then, to make our understanding of emptiness powerful enough to eliminate delusions quickly we meditate on the union of the two truths of our body – the non-dual body and its emptiness – continually until we gain deep experience of this meditation. Our meditation on emptiness will then have great power to eliminate our delusions, such as anger, attachment and self-grasping quickly. Then, when we distinguish between our body and its emptiness through their mere names, we will be free from extreme views that believe that the body either is inherently existent or does not exist at all.

This explanation of how to practise the four profundities of the aggregate of form can be applied to all other phenomena.

In the *Perfection of Wisdom Sutras*, Buddha explains a special training called 'training in dependent-related phenomena' through which we can understand emptiness correctly and easily, and complete our understanding of emptiness.

All things are dependent-related phenomena because they depend upon their causes, their name, their parts, their basis of imputation and their mere imputation by mind. Thus there are five ways in which a phenomenon can be dependent-related: a dependent-related phenomenon depending upon its causes, a dependent-related phenomenon depending upon its name, a dependent-related phenomenon depending upon its parts, a dependent-related phenomenon depending upon its basis of imputation and a dependent-related phenomenon depending upon its mere imputation by mind. Impermanent phenomena are dependent-related in all five ways, but permanent phenomena are dependent-related in only the last four ways.

What is a dependent-related phenomenon depending upon its causes? For example, at present we have this human body. We did not bring it from our former life, nobody gave it to us as a present and nobody created it for our use, but rather this body developed from its causes. The main causes of our human body are particular virtuous actions that we performed in our previous lives, such as moral discipline. It is through these actions that we have taken a human rebirth, and have this human body that gives us the opportunity to experience human conditions, receive a higher education, and especially attain liberation and enlightenment. Animals do not have such opportunities.

When we were conceived in the union of our father's sperm and our mother's ovum in our mother's womb, this union gradually transformed into our body and is therefore the substantial cause of our body. There were also many contributory conditions in the development of our body. It is therefore clear that our body depends upon its substantial cause and contributory conditions. When we realize this we should conclude, 'My body that I normally see as an independent entity does not exist at all because my actual body depends upon many causes and conditions.' Thinking in this way, we meditate on the mere absence of the independent body that we normally see; this is the emptiness of our body. We should practise this meditation continually until we gain a deep experience of this meditation.

We should also know that our body depends upon its name: if we search for our body, our body will disappear and only its name will remain. This indicates clearly that our body depends upon its name.

Our body also depends upon its parts. This is because there is no body other than its parts. When we realize this we should think, 'My body that I normally see as an independent entity does not exist at all because my actual body depends on its parts.' Thinking in this way we meditate on the mere absence of the independent body that we normally see.

When we realize that there is no body other than its parts we will realize that our body is just an imputation designated upon its basis of imputation, which is its parts. Therefore, it is clear that our body depends upon its basis of imputation. In this way, finally we will realize that our body depends upon mere imputation by a conceptual mind; it exists as mere imputation by mind. At this stage our understanding of the emptiness of our body is complete.

Among the five types of dependent-related phenomena, the first is the most gross dependent-related phenomena, the next three are progressively less gross, and the fifth is the most subtle dependent-related phenomena. When we realize the fifth type of dependent-related phenomena our understanding of the emptiness of our body is complete.

This explanation on how to train in dependent-related phenomena in relation to our body should be applied to our self, our world and all other things. In the Sutra called *Request by Yunkorkyong*, it says:

Because living beings do not understand emptiness,
In life and after life they wander in the cycle of
    suffering.
Therefore, the Compassionate Buddha gives hundreds
    of logical reasons
As methods to gain the realization of emptiness.

It is said that dependent-relationship is the king of all the logical reasons to establish emptiness that Buddha revealed in the Sutras.

THE EXPLANATION OF THE FOUR PROFUNDITIES OF THE AGGREGATES OF FEELING AND SO FORTH

Likewise, feeling, discrimination, compositional factors and consciousness are empty.

In this part of the Sutra, Avalokiteshvara advises us to know that feeling, discrimination, compositional factors and consciousness are empty of inherent existence in the same way as form is empty of inherent existence. In this way Avalokiteshvara encourages us to understand the emptiness of the five aggregates and to meditate on it. The five aggregates refer to our body and mind, which are the basis of imputation of our self.

In general it is important to distinguish between 'empty' and 'emptiness', as for many people they are the same. In Buddhism, 'empty' and 'emptiness' are very different. Emptiness is a very profound object; it is ultimate truth and the ultimate nature of phenomena. Understanding this emptiness brings great meaning to our life. However, an empty is just empty; knowing this does not bring any special meaning to our life. Emptiness of phenomena is a meaningful object, whereas an 'empty of phenomena' does not exist because phenomena pervade everywhere.

For us ordinary beings, our body and mind are the same as our self. This is because of the way in which we perceive them. For this reason, although this part of the Sutra encourages us to understand and meditate on the emptiness of our five aggregates, it principally encourages us to understand and meditate on the emptiness of our self. Normally, just through perceiving our self that we normally see we strongly think, for instance, 'My wish is so important.' In this way we develop attachment to the fulfilment of our wishes. In truth, our self that we normally see does not exist at all. To liberate ourself from suffering and problems we need to abandon our attachment to the fulfilment of our own wishes. This attachment is the source of all our daily problems. Since beginningless time, because we have been so attached to the fulfilment of our own wishes we have performed various kinds of non-virtuous actions – actions that harm others. As a result we continually experience various kinds of suffering and miserable conditions in life after life without end. When our wishes are not fulfilled we usually experience unpleasant feelings such as unhappiness or depression; this is our own problem because we are so attached to the fulfilment of our wishes. When we lose a close friend we experience pain and unhappiness, but this is only because of our attachment to this friend. When we lose our possessions, position or reputation we experience unhappiness and depression because we are so attached to these things. If we had no attachment there would be no basis to experience these problems. Many people are engaged in fighting, criminal actions and even warfare; all these actions arise from their strong attachment to the fulfilment of their own wishes. In this way we can see that there is not a single problem experienced by living beings that does not come from their attachment. This proves that unless we control our attachment our problems will never cease.

The method to abandon this attachment is meditation on the emptiness of our self – the mere absence of our self that we normally see. For this reason, Avalokiteshvara advises us that to abandon the source of all our problems and suffering we should understand and meditate on the emptiness of our self. If we put this advice into practice we will be permanently free from suffering and problems.

The explanation of the four profundities of the aggregate of form explained above can be applied to the four profundities of feeling, discrimination, compositional factors, consciousness and all other phenomena. By meditating on the four profundities of all phenomena we will first realize the emptiness of all phenomena with a subsequent valid cognizer and then with a direct valid cognizer. When we realize the emptiness of all phenomena with a non-conceptual direct valid cognizer we become a Superior being, or Arya in Sanskrit.

The Paths of Seeing, Meditation and No More Learning

Shariputra, like this all phenomena are emptiness, having no characteristics. They are not produced and do not cease. They have no defilement and no separation from defilement. They have no decrease and no increase.

In this part of the Sutra Avalokiteshvara says, 'Shariputra, like this all phenomena are emptiness.' This means that for Superior Bodhisattvas who are meditating on emptiness, all phenomena are emptiness; there are no conventional truths because the appearance of conventional truths has been dispelled by their dissolving their mind into emptiness. Because, initially, Superior Bodhisattvas are on the path of seeing, we can understand that this part of the Sutra reveals how to train in the perfection of wisdom on the path of seeing.

Avalokiteshvara says, '... having no characteristics. They are not produced and do not cease. They have no defilement and no separation from defilement. They have no decrease and no increase.' This means that because there are no conventional truths for Superior Bodhisattvas who are meditating on emptiness, it follows that for them there are no characteristics, no conventional nature, no production, no cessation, no defilement, no separation from defilement, no decrease and no increase – nothing exists other than emptiness. For such Superior Bodhisattvas all phenomena are gathered into emptiness; they abide in the vast space-like emptiness experiencing the deep inner peace of bliss.

A Superior Bodhisattva is a Bodhisattva who has attained a direct realization of emptiness. There are ten levels of Superior Bodhisattvas, from Bodhisattvas on the first ground to Bodhisattvas on the tenth ground, with each ground being progressively higher than the previous one. Initially the Bodhisattva on the first ground is on the path of seeing, but he or she then enters the path of meditation. The good qualities of Bodhisattvas on the first ground include the following: they have attained ultimate bodhichitta, they hold a close lineage of a Buddha Family, they have abandoned all intellectually-formed delusions, they no longer experience suffering or pain, they experience supreme joy in life after life, they can visit a hundred different worlds in one instant through their miracle powers, they can see directly a hundred former and future lives through their clairvoyance, they have the ability to engage in a hundred different concentrations in one instant, and they have abandoned actions that cause rebirth in samsara. They have such good qualities because of their realization of the perfection of wisdom of ultimate bodhichitta. We should deeply rejoice in their good qualities and make the determination to become like these Bodhisattvas.

We may wonder why it is necessary for us to understand these instructions on how to train in the perfection of wisdom since Avalokiteshvara is giving them to Bodhisattvas on the paths of accumulation, preparation, seeing and meditation, and we are not one of these Bodhisattvas. The answer is that because we have Buddha nature, the seed of becoming a Buddha, and we have met Buddhadharma, we have a great opportunity to attain the supreme happiness of enlightenment, which is the ultimate goal of our human life. To accomplish this ultimate goal we need to train in the Bodhisattva's paths of accumulation, preparation, seeing and meditation. There is no way to attain full enlightenment other than through this training. Although at present we may not be a Bodhisattva, we definitely need to apply effort to become one. Then we need to advance from path to path until we become an enlightened being. By our engaging in the practices of the Bodhisattva's paths of accumulation, preparation, seeing and meditation, our Buddha nature or seed will definitely ripen in our attaining enlightenment. This is the main reason why we need to understand and practise these teachings now. As mentioned before, Buddha's ultimate intention is to lead each and every living being to the state of enlightenment, and for this purpose he taught the *Perfection of Wisdom Sutras*.

Once we have attained the initial realization of ultimate bodhichitta, the actual way to train in the perfection of wisdom on the path of seeing is to improve this realization until it becomes the path of meditation by continually engaging in meditation on the emptiness of all phenomena, motivated by compassion for all living beings.

Akashagarbha

AN EXPLANATION OF HOW TO TRAIN IN THE
PERFECTION OF WISDOM ON THE PATH OF MEDITATION

Therefore, Shariputra, in emptiness there is no form, no feeling, no discrimination, no compositional factors, no consciousness. There is no eye, no ear, no nose, no tongue, no body, no mentality; no form, no sound, no smell, no taste, no tactile object, no phenomenon. There is no eye element and so forth up to no mentality element and also up to no element of mental consciousness. There is no ignorance and no exhaustion of ignorance and so forth up to no ageing and death and no exhaustion of ageing and death. Likewise, there is no suffering, origin, cessation or path; no exalted awareness, no attainment, and also no non-attainment.

This part of the Sutra reveals that the Bodhisattva on the first ground should advance from path to path until the tenth ground, which is the last 'station' from which the Bodhisattva will directly reach the ground of enlightenment, the final destination. He or she should do this by continually engaging in meditation on the emptiness of the five aggregates, the twelve sources, the eighteen elements, the twelve dependent-related links and the four noble truths.

The words 'in emptiness there is no form' reveal the emptiness of form, and '... no feeling' reveals the emptiness of feeling. The same can be applied to the remaining three aggregates, the twelve sources, the eighteen elements, the twelve dependent-related links and the four noble truths. In this way, we should know that this part of the Sutra reveals that the five aggregates, the twelve sources, the eighteen elements, the twelve dependent-related links and the four noble truths are the bases to establish emptiness. This has great meaning because it indirectly reveals the stages of the path to liberation or nirvana, which are common paths for both Hinayana and Mahayana. This is the hidden meaning of this part of the Sutra. The explanation of this hidden meaning has five parts:

1 Recognizing samsara
2 Who experiences suffering
3 How we experience suffering
4 How we wander in samsara
5 The attainment of liberation or nirvana

RECOGNIZING SAMSARA

Taking contaminated aggregates, in other words taking a contaminated body and mind, in life after life, is samsara. There are different ways of explaining samsara, as: contaminated aggregates, the cycle of contaminated rebirth, the cycle of uncontrolled death and rebirth, the cycle of impure life, or the cycle of the twelve dependent-related links. All these ways of explaining samsara are correct. For example, we take five contaminated aggregates in life after life without end, and this is our own samsara. To show this, Avalokiteshvara specifically explains the five aggregates as the bases upon which to establish emptiness.

WHO EXPERIENCES SUFFERING

Those who have attained liberation and enlightenment, and those who realize emptiness directly, do not experience suffering. Inanimate objects do not experience suffering because they have no feeling or discrimination. Only those who have taken contaminated aggregates – a contaminated body and mind – as their basis of imputation, experience suffering. This is another reason why Avalokiteshvara explains the five aggregates as the bases upon which to establish emptiness.

HOW WE EXPERIENCE SUFFERING

Because of our eye sense power, ear sense power and so forth meeting with their objects – forms, sounds and so forth – we develop an eye consciousness, ear consciousness and so forth that perceive inherently existent things. For us this automatically gives rise to a mind that believes these things to be inherently existent. This is our mind of self-grasping ignorance. Because of this ignorance we experience various kinds of sufferings and problems, which are mistaken appearances or hallucinations, just as we experience things in dreams. To show how suffering develops, Avalokiteshvara explains the twelve sources and eighteen elements as the bases upon which to establish emptiness.

HOW WE WANDER IN SAMSARA

We wander in samsara through experiencing the cycle of the twelve dependent-related links. This is not easy to understand unless we have studied teachings on them. The diagram of the Wheel of Life, which was designed by Buddha, shows how living beings are wandering in samsara through the cycle of twelve dependent-related links. An explanation of this diagram can be found in *Joyful Path of Good Fortune*.

A detailed explanation of the twelve sources, the eighteen elements and the twelve dependent-related links can be found in Appendix IV.

THE ATTAINMENT OF LIBERATION OR NIRVANA

The words 'Likewise, there is no suffering, origin, cessation or path' reveal the emptiness of suffering, origin, cessation and path, and thus indirectly reveal the practice of the four noble truths. In *Sutra of the Four Noble Truths*, Buddha says, 'You should know sufferings', which means that we should know the sufferings of our countless future lives and develop renunciation, the sincere wish to attain permanent liberation from them. He then says, 'You should abandon origins.' 'Origins' means delusions, principally self-grasping ignorance. Buddha is therefore encouraging us to abandon self-grasping ignorance, the root of all the sufferings of this life and of future lives. When Buddha then says, 'You should attain cessations', he is advising us to attain permanent liberation from all sufferings because temporary liberation from particular sufferings is not enough. And then when he says, 'You should practise the path', this means that to attain permanent liberation we need to meditate on the path to liberation, which is principally training in meditation on emptiness with the motivation of renunciation.

The words 'no exalted awareness, no attainment, and also no non-attainment' reveal the emptiness of exalted awareness, attainment and non-attainment. They indirectly reveal that exalted awareness, path and cessation are attainments; and that sufferings and origins are non-attainments, that is, objects we should abandon. 'Exalted awareness', 'spiritual path' and 'spiritual realization' are synonyms.

Renunciation is the gateway through which we enter the path to liberation, and bodhichitta is the gateway through which we enter the path to enlightenment. In summary, through applying effort to abandon the origin of suffering, self-grasping ignorance, by training in meditation on emptiness with the motivation of renunciation we will attain cessation, permanent liberation from suffering, and by training in meditation on emptiness with the motivation of bodhichitta we will attain full enlightenment.

Once we have attained the initial realization of the path of meditation, the actual way to train in the perfection of wisdom on the path of meditation is to improve this realization until it becomes the vajra-like concentration – which has the power to remove subtle mistaken appearance from our mind permanently – by continually engaging in meditation on the emptiness of all phenomena, motivated by compassion for all living beings.

AN EXPLANATION OF HOW TO ATTAIN
THE PATH OF NO MORE LEARNING

Therefore, Shariputra, because there is no attainment, Bodhisattvas rely upon and abide in the perfection of wisdom; their minds have no obstruction and no fear. Passing utterly beyond perversity, they attain the final nirvana. Also all the Buddhas who reside perfectly in the three times, having relied upon the perfection of wisdom, became manifest and complete Buddhas in the state of unsurpassed, perfect and complete enlightenment.

The meaning of this part of the Sutra is that Bodhisattvas on the path of meditation through continually meditating on the emptiness of attainment and of non-attainment – which means the emptiness of all phenomena – advance from path to path until they reach the tenth Bodhisattva ground. On the tenth ground the Bodhisattva will attain the realization of the higher perfection of wisdom called the 'vajra-like concentration'. In dependence upon this perfection of wisdom the Bodhisattva will be completely free from the fears of mistaken conceptions and the obstructions of mistaken appearances. In this way, the Bodhisattva will attain the final nirvana, the permanent cessation of subtle mistaken appearance. All the Buddhas of the past, present and future accomplish the unsurpassed attainment of full enlightenment, also known as the 'Path of No More Learning', in dependence upon this perfection of wisdom.

Conclusion

CONCLUSION

**Therefore, the mantra of the perfection of wisdom, the
mantra of great knowledge, the unsurpassed mantra,
the equal-to-the-unequalled mantra, the mantra that
thoroughly pacifies all suffering, since it is not false,
should be known as the truth. The mantra of the perfection of wisdom is proclaimed:**

**TAYATHA OM GATE GATE PARAGATE PARASAMGATE
BODHI SÖHA**

**Shariputra, a Bodhisattva, a Great Being, should
train in the profound perfection of wisdom like this.**

The meaning of this part of the Sutra is that in conclusion
we should understand and practise as follows. Mantra is an
inner realization that protects living beings from the obstructions of mistaken conceptions and mistaken appearances. In
this context, there are five types of mantra: the mantra of the
perfection of wisdom, the mantra of great knowledge, the
unsurpassed mantra, the equal-to-the-unequalled mantra,
and the unequalled mantra, or mantra that thoroughly pacifies all suffering.

The perfection of wisdom of the path of accumulation is called 'the mantra of the perfection of wisdom' because it is a wisdom mantra that is not associated with superior seeing observing emptiness. The perfection of wisdom of the path of preparation is called 'the mantra of great knowledge' because it is a wisdom mantra that is associated with superior seeing observing emptiness. The perfection of wisdom of the path of seeing is called 'the unsurpassed mantra' because it is a wisdom mantra that is associated with the direct realization of emptiness. The perfection of wisdom of the path of meditation is called 'the equal-to-the-unequalled mantra' because it is a wisdom mantra that is very close to attaining the unequalled mantra, actual enlightenment. The wisdom of enlightenment is called 'the unequalled mantra' because it has the power to pacify thoroughly the sufferings of all living beings.

The mantra that we verbally recite is not actual mantra but it is called 'mantra' because it principally reveals the wisdom mantra. An actual mantra is necessarily an inner realization.

We should know that training in the perfection of wisdom of the paths of accumulation, preparation, seeing, meditation and No More Learning are non-deceptive and truly meaningful practices. Understanding this we should make a strong determination, thinking, 'I must go for refuge to the Dharma of the perfection of wisdom of the paths of accumulation, preparation, seeing, meditation and No More Learning', and meditate on this determination. To make our determination strong and unchangeable we then recite the following verbal mantra while concentrating on its meaning:

TAYATHA OM GATE GATE PARAGATE PARASAMGATE
BODHI SÖHA

We should practise this meditation and recitation continually as our daily practice.

The meaning of this mantra is as follows: TAYATHA means 'Thus', OM refers to 'I', and GATE means 'go'. Together these words mean 'Thus I will go' or 'I will accomplish the perfection of wisdom of the path of accumulation.' The second GATE means 'I will accomplish the perfection of wisdom of the path of preparation', PARAGATE means 'I will accomplish the perfection of wisdom of the path of seeing', PARASAMGATE means 'I will accomplish the perfection of wisdom of the path of meditation', BODHI means 'I will accomplish the perfection of wisdom of the Path of No More Learning', and SÖHA means 'I will build the basic foundation for all these inner realizations to benefit all living beings.' Here, 'basic foundation' refers to training in the stages of the vast path, which is presented in Part Two.

Shariputra

Buddha's Approval and the Promise to Practise

THE APPROVAL OF THE ANSWERS BY BUDDHA

Then the Blessed One arose from that concentration and said to the Superior Avalokiteshvara, the Bodhisattva, the Great Being, that he had spoken well: 'Good, good, O Son of the lineage. It is like that. Since it is like that, just as you have revealed, in that way the profound perfection of wisdom should be practised, and the Tathagatas will also rejoice.'

As we know, when we are meditating single-pointedly we cannot talk or teach at the same time; to be able to talk or teach we need to arise from our concentration. However, because Buddhas realize ultimate truth and conventional truth directly and simultaneously they are able to talk or teach while single-pointedly meditating on emptiness; they do not need to arise from their concentration to do this. When Ananda says, 'Then the Blessed One arose from that concentration', he is saying this only following common appearance, the appearance of ordinary beings.

Also, as already mentioned, because this Sutra was taught by Buddha through his heart it is his own teaching. So when Buddha gives his approval to Avalokiteshvara's answers this is only following common appearance because the answer actually comes from Buddha himself.

THE FOLLOWERS ARE PLEASED AND TAKE THE TEACHINGS TO HEART

When the Blessed One had said this, the Venerable Shariputra, the Superior Avalokiteshvara, the Bodhisattva, the Great Being, and that entire circle of disciples as well as the worldly beings – gods, humans, demi-gods and spirits – were delighted and highly praised what had been spoken by the Blessed One.

When Buddha was giving teachings on the *Perfection of Wisdom Sutras*, the great assembly of disciples who received these teachings included humans, Bodhisattvas, gods, demi-gods and spirits. They all deeply rejoiced in their good fortune at having received this profound teaching and promised to practise and spread these teachings.

Among the human disciples, those with pure minds saw directly the non-human disciples such as the Deities Avalokiteshvara and Maitreya. The spirit disciples included the assembly of the naga disciples. It is said that at that time many of the naga kings had an especially strong devotion to Buddha's teachings on the *Perfection of Wisdom Sutras*, and after Buddha passed away, when for many reasons Mahayana Buddhism seriously degenerated, the naga spirits took the extensive scriptures of the *Perfection of Wisdom*

Sutras to their own world. Because of this, these scriptures disappeared from the human world for hundreds of years. Later, the great Master Nagarjuna visited the naga world to find these scriptures and return them to the human world. He then restored and spread Mahayana Buddhism in general and the teachings of the *Perfection of Wisdom Sutras* in particular. Therefore the great kindness of Nagarjuna is immeasurable. The Indian Buddhist master Atisha said:

We will attain the enlightenment of Buddhahood
By relying on the instructions that come from
    Nagarjuna and his disciple Chandrakirti;
With views that contradict these instructions, there is
    no attainment of enlightenment.

The life story of Nagarjuna can be found in Part Two.

Commentary to the *Heart Sutra*

PART TWO:
THE EXPLANATION OF THE HIDDEN
MEANING OF THE SUTRA

Ananda

Preliminary Explanation and the Lives of Protector Nagarjuna and Arya Asanga

PRELIMINARY EXPLANATION

We should know that each and every living being has their own body and mind, which are their subtle body and mind. These are called the 'continuously residing body and mind', and are his or her Buddha nature, the lineage of a future Buddha. Because they have this, when living beings meet Buddhadharma they will all finally attain the state of an enlightened Buddha.

An enlightened Buddha is a person who has woken from the sleep of ignorance, and whose function is to bestow peace of mind on each and every living being. When living beings experience peace of mind all the time they will always be happy; without peace of mind no one experiences happiness. Where does the peace of mind of living beings come from? It comes from their mind receiving Buddha's blessings. This is Buddha's function. From this we can understand that Buddha is the source of the happiness of all living beings. From our own experience we understand that in this impure life there is no real happiness or freedom at all. Therefore, because we and all living beings sincerely wish to be happy and free from suffering we definitely need to apply effort to attain the state of an enlightened Buddha. When we attain this state we will become the source of happiness for all other living beings. Buddha taught the *Heart Sutra* to lead all living beings to the supreme happiness of enlightenment.

This Sutra directly shows the stages of the profound path, but implicitly reveals the stages of the vast path. These two paths, profound and vast, are the actual path to enlightenment. The profound path is training in the perfection of wisdom, which has been explained in Part One; and the vast path is training in the paths of persons of initial and middling scopes, and the practices of love, compassion and bodhichitta.

Protector Nagarjuna received the instructions on the stages of the profound path from Bodhisattva Manjushri, who received them direct from Buddha Shakyamuni. Arya Asanga received the instructions of the stages of the vast path from Bodhisattva Maitreya, who received them direct from Buddha Shakyamuni. The lineages of these two instructions were passed from Teacher to Teacher in unbroken succession until they reached Atisha, the founder of Kadampa Buddhism. Atisha wrote a text called *Lamp for the Path* in which he explains the way to practise the stages of the profound and vast paths in a special presentation known as 'the stages of the path of persons of initial, middling and great scopes'. This includes, in a practical way, all Buddha's teachings on Sutra and Tantra.

The instructions that have this special presentation are called 'Kadam Lamrim' or 'Kadam Dharma'. Atisha's text

Lamp for the Path is the root text of Kadam Lamrim. It is very short, and without a detailed commentary to this text it is difficult to understand how to practise the stages of the profound and vast paths correctly, especially the stages of the profound path. Because of this, the wisdom of all Buddhas appeared in Tibet in the form of Je Tsongkhapa, who wrote extensive, middling and short commentaries to the *Lamp for the Path* and gave extensive public teachings. In this way, Kadam Lamrim flourished throughout Tibet, China, Mongolia and many other Asian countries, and now it is beginning to spread throughout the rest of the world. I personally have the opportunity to practise and to teach Kadam Dharma through the great kindness of Je Tsongkhapa and my Spiritual Guide Dorjechang Trijang Rinpoche, who is a manifestation of Je Tsongkhapa.

PROTECTOR NAGARJUNA

Nagarjuna's life and works were prophesied several times by Buddha. In a well-known passage in *Gone to Lanka Sutra* Buddha is asked who will uphold the doctrine after he has passed away. Buddha replies:

In the Southern region, in the Land of the Palms,
The monk Shriman of great renown,
Known by the name, 'Naga',
Will refute the extremes of existence and non-
    existence.
Having proclaimed to the world my teachings,
The unsurpassed Great Vehicle,
He will accomplish the ground, Very Joyful,
And depart to the Land of Bliss.

As predicted, four hundred years after Buddha passed away, a son was born to a prosperous Brahmin family living in an area of Southern India known as Bedarwa, or the 'Land of the Palms'. An oracle predicted that the child would live for only seven days, but that his life span could be extended by a further seven days if gifts were bestowed upon a hundred ordinary people, by a further seven months if offerings were made to a hundred brahmins, or by a further seven years if offerings were made to a hundred monks. However, the oracle knew of no method to extend his life beyond that. Accordingly, his parents made offerings to a hundred monks, and as a result were able to live happily with their son for seven years.

As the child's seventh birthday drew near, however, they sent him on a pilgrimage with several of their servants, for they could not bear to witness his death. Guided by a manifestation of Avalokiteshvara, the party made its way to Nalanda Monastery where they met the great Teacher Saraha. They explained the boy's plight to Saraha, and he told them that the child could avert an untimely death by staying at Nalanda and taking ordination as a monk. He gave the child an empowerment into the long-life practice of Buddha Amitayus and encouraged him to practise that yoga extensively. On the eve of his seventh birthday the child recited the mantra of Amitayus without interruption and as a result averted an untimely death. The following day he was ordained as a monk and given the name 'Shrimanta'. He remained at Nalanda where under the protection of Manjushri he was able to study all the Sutras and Tantras. He soon became a fully-accomplished scholar and Teacher, and his reputation spread widely. Eventually he was appointed Abbot of Nalanda.

Nagarjuna's life comprised three great periods of auspicious deeds that correspond to Buddha's three turnings of the Wheel of Dharma, which is why he is often referred to as 'the Second Buddha'. The first period was during his tenure as Abbot of Nalanda. Unfortunately, the moral discipline of the monks had degenerated since the time Buddha first gave the vows, and Nagarjuna was very active in restoring the purity of the discipline. He clarified many points of moral discipline in extensive teachings and composed a number of works on pure conduct. These writings, known as the *Collection of Advice*, include such works as *Precious Garland*, *Friendly Letter*, *Tree of Wisdom*, *A Hundred Wisdoms* and *Drops for Healing Beings*. These activities are likened to Buddha's first turning of the Wheel of Dharma.

Nagarjuna is best remembered, however, for the works of the second period. As mentioned before, not long after Buddha passed away, the *Perfection of Wisdom Sutras*, the principal Mahayana teachings, disappeared from this world. It is said this is because some nagas who had received this teaching from Buddha had taken the extensive *Perfection of Wisdom* scriptures to their own world for safekeeping. There remained only a few practitioners who could understand these teachings, and most of them kept their practice secret. The only teachings of Buddha to remain widespread were the Hinayana teachings, and as a result many people assumed that these were the only teachings Buddha had given. Some time later the nagas invited Nagarjuna to visit them and returned the *Perfection of Wisdom* scriptures to him. Nagarjuna brought the scriptures to the human world and propagated them widely. Because of his special relationship with the nagas, and because he cured many nagas of sickness by means of special ritual prayers, Nagarjuna was given the name 'Protector of the nagas'. 'Arjuna' was added to his name because he spread the Mahayana teachings with great speed and accuracy, just as the legendary archer Arjuna had delivered arrows from his bow. Hence he finally became known as 'Protector Nagarjuna'.

Because he had a very lucid mind and great wisdom Nagarjuna was able perfectly to understand the *Perfection of Wisdom Sutras* and explain them to others. He spread these teachings widely, thus instigating a great revival of the Mahayana doctrine in this world. He presented a system of reasoning which, because it steers a flawless course between the two extremes of existence and non-existence, became known as the 'Philosophy of the Middle Way', or 'Madhyamaka'. Nagarjuna composed many commentaries to the *Perfection of Wisdom Sutras* that elucidate the Madhyamaka view. These treatises, known as the *Collection of Reasonings*, include the famous *Fundamental Wisdom of the Middle Way*, and its four limbs: *Sixty Reasonings*, *Seventy Emptinesses*, *Finely Woven* and *Refutation of Objections*. He also wrote *Compendium of Sutras*, *Five Stages of the Completion Stage of Guhyasamaja* and many other commentaries to the Sutras and Tantras. These activities are likened to Buddha's second turning of the Wheel of Dharma.

Nagarjuna's third period of auspicious deeds took place towards the end of his life. Acting on advice from Tara, he returned to Southern India and dwelt at a place called Mount Splendour, where he gave further extensive teachings on both the Sutras and Tantras and composed many more texts. These writings, known as the *Collection of Praises*, include such works as *Praise of the Dharmadhatu*, *Praise of the Supramundane*, *Praise of the Inconceivable* and *Praise of the*

Ultimate. These activities are likened to Buddha's third turning of the Wheel of Dharma.

It is not possible in such a brief account even to begin to do justice to Nagarjuna's life and works. Throughout his life he devoted himself entirely to reviving the Mahayana Dharma and sustaining the Mahayana Sangha. To this end he gave prolific teachings, composed many books on Sutra and Tantra, and performed countless other excellent deeds. As mentioned in *Gone to Lanka Sutra*, Nagarjuna had accomplished the realization of the Bodhisattva's first ground, called 'Very Joyful'. He then advanced further and finally reached the land of the supreme bliss of enlightenment.

ARYA ASANGA

Asanga was a great practitioner who had a sincere wish to receive teachings on the *Perfection of Wisdom Sutras*, in which he would find all the instructions on the stages of the path to enlightenment. He tried to find a Teacher who would teach him the hidden meaning of the *Perfection of Wisdom Sutras*, that is, the stages of the vast path, but he could not find such a Teacher anywhere. Finally Asanga decided he needed to attain a direct vision of Maitreya, who had received these teachings directly from Buddha Shakyamuni. To accomplish this aim Asanga engaged in retreat in a remote mountain cave. For three years he concentrated on the visualization, meditation and recitation of the mantra of Buddha Maitreya, but his karmic obstructions prevented him from seeing Maitreya and he became discouraged and stopped his retreat. As he was returning to his home he met a man working very hard at cutting a block of iron with a peacock feather. Asanga asked the man, 'How can you cut this iron block with a peacock feather?' The man replied, 'With effort we can accomplish anything. Look, I have already made some progress', and he showed Asanga a mark on the block. Asanga then asked, 'What are you going to do when you have cut it?' and the man replied, 'Nothing. Just leave it here.' Asanga thought 'If this man can work so very hard for something that has no meaning, surely I can work continually in my retreat for something that will bring great meaning for myself and countless living beings?' With this thought, he returned to his retreat.

The man cutting the iron block with the peacock feather was in fact emanated by Maitreya for Asanga's benefit. Through this and many other emanations Maitreya continually helped Asanga. After twelve years of retreat Asanga again became discouraged and abandoned his retreat, so Maitreya emanated as a female dog that had collapsed on the roadside and was being slowly eaten alive by many maggots. When Asanga saw the dog he developed strong compassion for both the dog and the maggots. To save the lives of both, he cut a piece of flesh from his thigh and, taking all the maggots from the dog's body with his tongue, transferred them to the piece of his flesh. Through these compassionate virtuous actions, the karmic obstructions that had prevented him from seeing Maitreya were completely purified and instead of seeing the dog Asanga suddenly saw Maitreya. With a feeling of both shock and joy Asanga exclaimed, 'Why did I need to wait such a long time to see you?' Maitreya replied, 'I have been with you from the very beginning of your retreat, but your karmic mental obstructions prevented you from seeing me. Now, how can I help you?'

Asanga then requested Maitreya, 'Please give me the instructions of the *Perfection of Wisdom Sutras* that you received direct from Buddha Shakyamuni so that I can attain Buddha's enlightenment as you did.' Then, through the power of Maitreya's blessings, Asanga instantaneously reached Maitreya's Yiga Chodzin Palace in Tushita Pure Land, and there received the instructions on the *Perfection of Wisdom Sutra*.

Asanga also received instructions on Maitreya's *Five Sets of Dharma*, which comprise *Ornament of Clear Realization* (a commentary to the *Perfection of Wisdom Sutras*), and four commentaries to other Sutra teachings of Buddha – *Ornament for Mahayana Sutras*, *Explanation of Phenomena and Emptiness of Phenomena*, *Distinguishing the Middle Way and the Extremes*, and *Sublime Continuum*.

Asanga stayed in Tushita Pure Land for fifty years. During this time he emphasized the practice of the stages of the path to enlightenment that he had received directly from Maitreya, and progressed to the third ground of a Superior Bodhisattva. He also translated Maitreya's *Five Sets of Dharma* from the language of Tushita Pure Land into Sanskrit, and then returned to the human world carrying these five texts.

At that time there were many famous scholars and teachers, including Asanga's younger brother Vasubandhu, who denied Buddha's Mahayana teachings. Vasubandhu was originally a famous Hinayana Teacher who had thousands of disciples. In one book he criticized the Mahayana, saying that it was like a flower in the sky that did not exist, that Nagarjuna was one of the messengers of the maras, and that his own brother Asanga was a follower of maras.

Asanga found it hard to bear his younger brother creating so much negative karma, and out of compassion thought of ways of stopping him. Finally he decided to ask a Mahayana practitioner who had memorized the Mahayana Sutra called *Sutra on the Ten Grounds (of a Bodhisattva)* to visit his younger brother, and while staying there to recite this Sutra out aloud early every morning. The practitioner went to see Vasubandhu and, since he had been sent by his older brother, Vasubandhu let him stay. Early the next morning the practitioner recited the Sutra out aloud, and Vasubandhu listened. Because he was so intelligent and had a such a sharp scholarly mind he began to appreciate this Mahayana Sutra and developed a good feeling for it. The next morning the practitioner again recited the Sutra, and Vasubandhu listened carefully and easily understood its real meaning. He developed deep appreciation for it, and began to regret his previous denial of Buddha's Mahayana teachings as well as his criticism of Nagarjuna and his older brother. On the third morning when the practitioner recited the Sutra Vasubandhu gained a deep understanding of its entire meaning.

He thought how wonderful and precious were Buddha's teachings on the Bodhisattva's way of life, and developed such a deep regret for having denied Buddha's Mahayana teachings and such an intense wish to purify the effects of his negativities that he became almost crazed. He took a knife and asked everyone he met to cut out his tongue! When people asked him why, he replied, 'With this tongue I created such heavy evil actions that I want to die. I want to purify these actions now, so please cut out my tongue.' One person told Vasubandhu that to purify his negative karma he did not need to cut out his tongue but should visit his brother Asanga, who would teach him a special method for purifying his negativity. With tears of regret Vasubandhu requested his brother, 'Please teach me a method for purifying my negative karma.' Asanga was able to communicate direct with Buddha Maitreya and told his brother to wait while he asked Maitreya what kind of purification his younger brother should do. Maitreya told Asanga that if Vasubandhu immediately entered the Mahayana path and wrote many commentaries to Mahayana Sutras his negative karma would gradually be purified. When Asanga told his brother what Maitreya had said, Vasubandhu immediately entered the Mahayana path and became a disciple of Asanga, later writing many commentaries to Mahayana Sutras. In this way he basically purified his negative karma, but because subtle imprints of his negativity still remained it took longer for Vasubandhu to attain enlightenment than it would otherwise have done.

Asanga passed the instructions of the stages of the vast path to his disciples, principally to Vasubandhu. In time these instructions reached Atisha, who, as already mentioned, taught a special presentation of Lamrim known as 'the stages of the path of persons of initial, middling and great scopes'. For this reason Atisha is renowned as the founder of Kadam Lamrim. Atisha based his Lamrim instructions on Maitreya's *Ornament for Clear Realization*, which Asanga had translated from the language of Tushita Heaven into Sanskrit.

Nagarjuna

The Path of a Person of
Initial Scope

THE STAGES OF THE VAST PATH:
THE HIDDEN MEANING OF THE *HEART SUTRA*

Having understood how to train in the perfection of wisdom as explained in Part One, if we learn how to train in the stages of the vast path we will know the entire meaning of the *Heart Sutra*. Therefore, in this commentary there now follows a presentation of the stages of the vast path. This has three parts:

1 The path of a person of initial scope
2 The path of a person of middling scope
3 The path of a person of great scope

THE PATH OF A PERSON OF INITIAL SCOPE

In this context, a 'person of initial scope' refers to someone who has an initial capacity for developing spiritual understanding and realizations.

THE PRECIOUSNESS OF OUR HUMAN LIFE

The purpose of understanding the preciousness of our human life is to encourage ourself to take the real meaning of our human life and not to waste it in meaningless activities. Our human life is very precious and meaningful, but only if we use it to attain permanent liberation and the supreme happiness of enlightenment. We should encourage ourself to accomplish the real meaning of our human life through understanding and contemplating the following explanation.

Many people believe that material development is the real meaning of human life, but we can see that no matter how much material development there is in the world it never reduces human suffering and problems. Instead, it often causes suffering and problems to increase; therefore it is not the real meaning of human life. We should know that at present we have reached the human world for just a brief moment from our former lives, and we have the opportunity to attain the supreme happiness of enlightenment through practising Dharma. This is our extraordinary good fortune. When we attain enlightenment we will have fulfilled our own wishes, and we can fulfil the wishes of all other living beings; we will have liberated ourself permanently from the sufferings of this life and countless future lives, and we can directly benefit each and every living being every day. The attainment of enlightenment is therefore the real meaning of human life.

Enlightenment is the inner light of wisdom that is permanently free from all mistaken appearance, and whose function is to bestow mental peace upon each and every living being every day. Right now we have obtained a human rebirth and have the opportunity to attain enlightenment through Dharma practice, so if we waste this precious opportunity in meaningless activities there is no greater loss and no greater foolishness. This is because in future such a precious opportunity will be extremely hard to find. In one Sutra Buddha illustrates this by giving the following analogy. He asks his disciples, 'Suppose there existed a vast and deep ocean the size of this world, and on its surface there floated a golden yoke, and at the bottom of the ocean there lived a blind turtle who surfaced only once in every one hundred thousand years. How often would that turtle raise its head through the middle of the yoke?' His disciple, Ananda, answers that, indeed, it would be extremely rare.

In this context, the vast and deep ocean refers to samsara – the cycle of impure life that we have experienced since beginningless time, continually in life after life without end – the golden yoke refers to Buddhadharma, and the blind turtle refers to us. Although we are not physically a turtle, mentally we are not much different; and although our physical eyes may not be blind, our wisdom eyes are. For most of our countless previous lives we have remained at the bottom of the ocean of samsara, in the three lower realms – the animal, hungry ghost and hell realms – surfacing only once in every one hundred thousand years or so as a human being. Even when we briefly reach the upper realm of samsara's ocean as a human being, it is extremely rare to meet the golden yoke of Buddhadharma: the ocean of samsara is extremely vast, the golden yoke of Buddhadharma does not remain in one place but moves from place to place, and our wisdom eyes are always blind. For these reasons, Buddha says that in the future, even if we obtain a human rebirth, it will be extremely rare to meet Buddhadharma again; meeting Kadam Dharma is even more rare than this. We can see that the great majority of human beings in the world, even though they have briefly reached the upper realm of samsara as human beings, have not met Buddhadharma. This is because their wisdom eyes have not opened.

What does 'meeting Buddhadharma' mean? It means entering into Buddhism by sincerely seeking refuge in Buddha, Dharma and Sangha, and thus having the opportunity to enter and make progress on the path to enlightenment. If we do not meet Buddhadharma we have no opportunity to do this, and therefore we have no opportunity to accomplish the pure and everlasting happiness of enlightenment, the real meaning of human life. In conclusion, we should think:

At present I have briefly reached the human world and have the opportunity to attain permanent liberation from suffering and the supreme happiness of enlightenment through putting Dharma into practice. If I waste this precious opportunity in meaningless activities there is no greater loss and no greater foolishness.

With this thought we make the strong determination to practise the Dharma of Buddha's teachings on renunciation, universal compassion and the profound view of emptiness now, while we have the opportunity. We then meditate on this determination again and again. We should practise this contemplation and meditation every day in many sessions, and in this way encourage ourself to take the real meaning of our human life.

We should ask ourself what we consider to be most important – what do we wish for, strive for, or daydream about? For some people it is material possessions, such as a large house with all the latest luxuries, a fast car or a well-paid job. For others it is reputation, good looks, power, excitement or adventure. Many try to find the meaning of their life in relationships with their family and circle of friends. All these things can make us superficially happy for a short while but they will also cause us much worry and suffering. They will never give us the real happiness that all of us, in our hearts, long for. Since we cannot take them with us when we die, if we have made them the principal meaning of our life they will eventually let us down. As an end in themselves worldly attainments are hollow; they are not the real meaning of human life.

With our human life we can attain the supreme permanent peace of mind, known as 'nirvana', and enlightenment by putting Dharma into practice. Since these attainments are non-deceptive and ultimate states of happiness they are the real meaning of human life. However, because our desire for worldly enjoyment is so strong, we have little or no interest in Dharma practice. From a spiritual point of view, this lack of interest in Dharma practice is a type of laziness called the 'laziness of attachment'. For as long as we have this laziness, the door to liberation will be closed to us, and consequently we will continue to experience misery and suffering in this life and in countless future lives. The way to overcome this laziness, the main obstacle to our Dharma practice, is to meditate on death.

We need to contemplate and meditate on our death again and again until we gain a deep realization of death. Although on an intellectual level we all know that eventually we are going to die, our awareness of death remains superficial. Since our intellectual knowledge of death does not touch our hearts, each and every day we continue to think 'I will not die today, I will not die today.' Even on the day of our death, we are still thinking about what we will do tomorrow or next week. This mind that thinks every day 'I will not die today' is deceptive – it leads us in the wrong direction and causes our human life to become empty. On the other hand, through meditating on death we will gradually replace the deceptive thought 'I will not die today' with the non-deceptive thought 'I may die today.' The mind that spontaneously thinks each and every day 'I may die today' is the realization of death. It is this realization that directly eliminates our laziness of attachment and opens the door to the spiritual path.

In general, we may die today or we may not die today – we do not know. However, if we think each day 'I may not die today', this thought will deceive us because it comes from our ignorance; whereas if instead we think each day 'I may die today', this thought will not deceive us because it comes from our wisdom. This beneficial thought will prevent our laziness of attachment, and will encourage us to prepare for the welfare of our countless future lives or to put great effort into entering the path to liberation and enlightenment. In this way, we will make our present human life meaningful. Until now we have wasted our countless former lives without any meaning; we have brought nothing with us from our former lives except delusions and suffering.

WHAT DOES OUR DEATH MEAN?

Our death is the permanent separation of our body and mind. We may experience many temporary separations of our body and mind, but these are not our death. For example, when those who have completed their training in the practice known as 'transference of consciousness' engage in meditation, their mind separates from their body. Their body remains where they are meditating, and their mind goes to a Pure Land and then returns to their body. At night, during dreams, our body remains in bed but our mind goes to various places of the dream world and then returns to our body. These separations of our body and mind are not our death because they are only temporary.

At death our mind separates from our body permanently. Our body remains at the place of this life but our mind goes to various places of our future lives, like a bird leaving one nest and flying to another. This clearly shows the existence of our countless future lives, and that the nature and function of our body and mind are very different. Our body is a visual form that possesses colour and shape, but our mind is a formless continuum that always lacks colour and shape. The nature of our mind is empty like space, and its function is to perceive or understand objects. Through this we can understand that our brain is not our mind. The brain is simply a part of our body that, for example, can be photographed, whereas our mind cannot.

We may not be happy to hear about our death, but contemplating and meditating on death is very important for the effectiveness of our Dharma practice. This is because it prevents the main obstacle to our Dharma practice – the laziness of attachment to the things of this life – and it encourages us to practise pure Dharma right now. If we do this we will accomplish the real meaning of human life before our death.

Asanga

HOW TO MEDITATE ON DEATH

First we engage in the following contemplation:

I will definitely die. There is no way to prevent my body from finally decaying. Day by day, moment by moment, my life is slipping away. I have no idea when I will die; the time of death is completely uncertain. Many young people die before their parents, some die the moment they are born – there is no certainty in this world. Furthermore, there are so many causes of untimely death. The lives of many strong and healthy people are destroyed by accidents. There is no guarantee that I will not die today.

Having repeatedly contemplated these points, we mentally repeat over and over again 'I may die today, I may die today', and concentrate on the feeling it evokes. We transform our mind into this feeling 'I may die today' and remain on it single-pointedly for as long as possible. We should practise this meditation repeatedly until we spontaneously believe each and every day 'I may die today'. Eventually we will come to a conclusion: 'Since I will soon have to depart from this world, there is no sense in my becoming attached to the things of this life. Instead, from now on I will devote my whole life to practising Dharma purely and sincerely.' We then maintain this determination day and night.

During the meditation break, without laziness we should apply effort to our Dharma practice. Realizing that worldly pleasures are deceptive, and that they distract us from using our life in a meaningful way, we should abandon attachment to them. In this way, we can eliminate the main obstacle to pure Dharma practice.

THE DANGERS OF LOWER REBIRTH

The purpose of this explanation is to encourage us to prepare protection from the dangers of lower rebirth. If we do not do this now, while we have a human life with its freedoms and endowments and we have the opportunity to do so, it will be too late once we have taken any of the three lower rebirths; and it will be extremely difficult to obtain such a precious human life again. It is said to be easier for human beings to attain enlightenment than it is for beings such as animals to attain a precious human rebirth. Understanding this will encourage us to abandon non-virtue, or negative actions, to practise virtue, or positive actions, and to seek refuge in Buddha, Dharma and Sangha (the supreme spiritual friends); this is our actual protection.

Performing non-virtuous actions is the main cause of taking lower rebirth, whereas practising virtue and seeking refuge in Buddha, Dharma and Sangha are the main causes of taking a precious human rebirth – a rebirth in which we have the opportunity to attain permanent liberation from all suffering. Heavy non-virtuous actions are the main cause of rebirth as a hell being, middling non-virtuous actions are the main cause of rebirth as a hungry ghost, and lesser non-virtuous actions are the main cause of rebirth as an animal. There are many examples given in Buddhist scriptures of how non-virtuous actions lead to rebirth in the three lower realms.

There was once a hunter whose wife came from a family of animal farmers. After he died he took rebirth as a cow belonging to his wife's family. A butcher then bought this cow, slaughtered it and sold the meat. The hunter was reborn seven times as a cow belonging to the same family, and in this way became food for other people.

In Tibet there is a lake called Yamdroktso, where many people from the nearby town used to spend their whole lives fishing. At one time a great Yogi with clairvoyance visited the town and said, 'I see the people of this town and the fish in this lake are continually switching their positions.' What he meant was that the people of the town who enjoyed fishing were reborn as the fish, the food of other people, and the fish in the lake were reborn as the people who enjoyed fishing. In this way, changing their physical aspect, they were continually killing and eating each other. This cycle of misery continued from generation to generation.

HOW TO MEDITATE ON THE DANGERS OF LOWER REBIRTH

First we engage in the following contemplation:

When the oil of an oil lamp is exhausted, the flame goes out because the flame is produced from the oil; but when our body dies our consciousness is not extinguished, because consciousness is not produced from the body. When we die our mind has to leave this present body, which is just a temporary abode, and find another body, rather like a bird leaving one nest to fly to another. Our mind has no freedom to remain and no choice about where to go. We are blown to the place of our next rebirth by the winds of our actions or karma (our good fortune or misfortune). If the karma that ripens at our death time is negative, we will definitely take a lower rebirth. Heavy negative karma causes rebirth in hell, middling negative karma causes rebirth as a hungry ghost and lesser negative karma causes rebirth as an animal.

It is very easy to commit heavy negative karma. For example, simply by swatting a mosquito out of anger we create the cause to be reborn in hell. Throughout this and all our countless previous lives we have committed many heavy negative actions. Unless we have already purified these actions by practising sincere confession, their potentialities remain in our mental continuum, and any one of these negative potentialities could ripen when we die. Bearing this in mind, we should ask ourself, 'If I die today, where will I be tomorrow? It is quite possible that I will find myself in the animal realm, among the hungry ghosts, or in hell. If someone were to call me a stupid cow today, I would find it difficult to bear, but what will I do if I actually become a cow, a pig, or a fish – the food of human beings?'

Having repeatedly contemplated these points and understood how beings in the lower realms, such as animals, experience suffering, we generate a strong fear of taking rebirth in the lower realms. This feeling of fear is the object of our meditation. We then hold this without forgetting it; our mind should remain on this feeling of fear single-pointedly for as long as possible. If we lose the object of our meditation we renew the feeling of fear by immediately remembering it or by repeating the contemplation.

During the meditation break we try never to forget our feeling of fear of taking rebirth in the lower realms. In general, fear is meaningless, but the fear generated through the above contemplation and meditation has immense meaning, as it arises from wisdom and not from ignorance. This fear is the main cause of seeking refuge in Buddha, Dharma and Sangha, which is the actual protection from such dangers, and helps us to be mindful and conscientious in avoiding non-virtuous actions.

GOING FOR REFUGE

In this context, 'going for refuge' means seeking refuge in Buddha, Dharma and Sangha. The purpose of this practice is to protect ourself permanently from taking lower rebirth. At present, because we are human, we are free from rebirth as an animal, hungry ghost or hell being, but this is only temporary. We are like a prisoner who gets permission to stay at home for a week, but then has to return to prison. We need permanent liberation from the sufferings of this life and countless future lives. This depends upon entering, making progress on and completing the Buddhist path to liberation, which in turn depends upon entering Buddhism.

We enter Buddhism through the practice of going for refuge. For our practice of refuge to be qualified, while visualizing Buddha in front of us we should verbally or mentally make the promise to seek refuge in Buddha, Dharma and Sangha throughout our life. This promise is our refuge vow, and is the gateway through which we enter Buddhism. For as long as we keep this promise we are inside Buddhism, but if we break this promise we are outside. By entering and remaining inside Buddhism we have the opportunity to begin, make progress on and complete the Buddhist path to liberation and enlightenment.

We should never give up our promise to seek refuge in Buddha, Dharma and Sangha throughout our life. Going for refuge to Buddha, Dharma and Sangha means that we apply effort to receiving Buddha's blessings, to putting Dharma into practice and to receiving help from Sangha. These are the three principal commitments of the refuge vow. Through maintaining and sincerely practising these three principal commitments of refuge we can fulfil our final goal.

Atisha

The main reason why we need to make the determination and promise to seek refuge in Buddha, Dharma and Sangha throughout our life is that we need to attain permanent liberation from suffering. At present we may be free from physical suffering and mental pain, but as mentioned earlier this freedom is only temporary. Later in this life and in our countless future lives we will have to experience unbearable physical suffering and mental pain continually, in life after life without end.

When our life is in danger or we are threatened by someone, we usually seek refuge in the police. Of course, sometimes the police can protect us from a particular danger, but they cannot give us permanent liberation from death. When we are seriously ill we seek refuge in doctors. Sometimes doctors can cure a particular illness, but no doctor can give us permanent liberation from sickness. What we really need is permanent liberation from all sufferings, and as human beings we can achieve this by seeking refuge in Buddha, Dharma and Sangha.

Buddhas are 'awakened', which means that they have awakened from the sleep of ignorance and are free from the dreams of samsara, the cycle of impure life. They are completely pure beings who are permanently free from all delusions and mistaken appearance. As mentioned earlier, Buddha's function is to bestow mental peace on each and every living being every day by giving blessings. We know that we are happy when our mind is peaceful, and unhappy when it is not. It is therefore clear that our happiness depends upon our having a peaceful mind and not on good external conditions. Even if our external conditions are poor, if we maintain a peaceful mind all the time we will always be happy. Through continually receiving Buddha's blessings we can maintain a peaceful mind all the time. Buddha is therefore the source of our happiness. Dharma is the actual protection through which we are permanently released from the sufferings of sickness, ageing, death and rebirth; and Sangha are the supreme spiritual friends who guide us to correct spiritual paths. Through these three precious wishful-filling jewels, Buddha, Dharma and Sangha – known as the 'Three Jewels' – we can fulfil our own wishes as well as the wishes of all living beings.

Every day from the depths of our heart we should recite requesting prayers to the enlightened Buddhas, while maintaining deep faith in them. This is a simple method for us to receive the Buddhas' blessings continually. We should also join group prayers, known as 'pujas', organized at Buddhist Temples or Prayer Halls, which are powerful methods to receive the Buddhas' blessings and protection.

HOW TO MEDITATE ON GOING FOR REFUGE

First we engage in the following contemplation:

I want to protect and liberate myself permanently from the sufferings of this life and countless future lives. I can accomplish this only by receiving Buddha's blessings, putting Dharma into practice and receiving help from Sangha – the supreme spiritual friends.

Thinking deeply in this way, we first make the strong determination and then the promise to seek refuge sincerely in Buddha, Dharma and Sangha throughout our life. We should meditate on this determination every day and maintain our promise continually for the rest of our life. As the commitments of our refuge vow we should always apply effort to receiving Buddha's blessings, to putting Dharma into practice and to receiving help from Sangha, our pure spiritual friends including our Spiritual Teacher. This is how we go for refuge to Buddha, Dharma and Sangha. Through this we will accomplish our aim – permanent liberation from all the sufferings of this life and countless future lives, the real meaning of our human life.

To maintain our promise to go for refuge to Buddha, Dharma and Sangha throughout our life, and so that we and all living beings may receive Buddha's blessings and protection, we recite the following refuge prayer every day with strong faith:

I and all sentient beings, until we achieve enlightenment,
Go for refuge to Buddha, Dharma and Sangha.

WHAT IS KARMA?

The purpose of understanding and believing in karma is to prevent future suffering and to establish the basic foundation for the path to liberation and enlightenment. Generally, karma means 'action'. From non-virtuous actions comes suffering and from virtuous actions comes happiness: if we believe this, we believe in karma. Buddha gave extensive teachings that prove the truth of this statement, and many different examples that show the special connection between the actions of our former lives and our experiences of this life, some of which are explained in *Joyful Path of Good Fortune*.

In our previous lives we performed various kinds of non-virtuous actions that caused others suffering. As a result of these non-virtuous actions, various kinds of miserable conditions and situations arise and we experience endless human suffering and problems. This is the same for all other living beings.

We should judge whether or not we believe that the main cause of suffering is our non-virtuous actions and the main cause of happiness is our virtuous actions. If we do not believe this we will never apply effort to accumulating virtuous actions, or merit, and we will never purify our non-virtuous actions, and because of this we will experience suffering and difficulties continually, in life after life without end.

Every action we perform leaves an imprint on our very subtle mind, and each imprint eventually gives rise to its own effect. Our mind is like a field, and performing actions is like sowing seeds in that field. Virtuous actions sow seeds of future happiness and non-virtuous actions sow seeds of future suffering. These seeds remain dormant in our mind until the conditions for them to ripen occur, and then they produce their effect. In some cases, this can happen many lifetimes after the original action was performed.

The seeds that ripen when we die are very important because they determine what kind of rebirth we will take in our next life. Which particular seed ripens at death depends upon the state of mind in which we die. If we die with a peaceful mind, this will stimulate a virtuous seed and we will experience a fortunate rebirth. However, if we die with an unpeaceful mind, such as in a state of anger, this will stimulate a non-virtuous seed and we will experience an unfortunate rebirth. This is similar to the way in which nightmares are triggered by our being in an agitated state of mind just before falling asleep.

All inappropriate actions, including killing, stealing, sexual misconduct, lying, divisive speech, hurtful speech, idle chatter, covetousness, malice and holding wrong views, are non-virtuous actions. When we abandon non-virtuous actions and apply effort to purifying our previous non-virtuous actions we are practising moral discipline. This will prevent us from experiencing future suffering and from taking a lower rebirth. Examples of virtuous actions are training in all the meditations and other spiritual practices presented in this book. Meditation is a virtuous mental action that is the main cause for experiencing mental peace in the future. Whenever we practise meditation, whether or not our meditation is clear, we are performing a virtuous mental action that is a cause of our future happiness and peace of mind. We are normally concerned mainly about bodily and verbal actions, but in reality mental actions are more important. Our bodily and verbal actions depend upon our mental action – upon our mentally making a decision.

Whenever we perform virtuous actions such as meditation or other spiritual practices we should have the following mental determination:

While riding the horse of virtuous actions
I will guide it into the path of liberation with the reins
of renunciation;
And through urging this horse onward with the whip
of effort,
I will quickly reach the Pure Land of liberation and
enlightenment.

Having contemplated the above explanation, we should think:

Since I myself never wish to suffer and always want to be happy, I must abandon and purify my non-virtuous actions and sincerely perform virtuous actions.

We should meditate on this determination every day, and put our determination into practice.

Je Tsongkhapa

The Path of a Person of Middling Scope

In this context, a 'person of middling scope' refers to someone who has a middling capacity for developing spiritual understanding and realizations.

WHAT WE SHOULD KNOW

As mentioned previously, in *Sutra of the Four Noble Truths* Buddha says, 'You should know sufferings.' In saying this Buddha is advising us that we should know about the unbearable sufferings that we will experience in our countless future lives, and therefore develop renunciation, the determination to liberate ourself permanently from these sufferings.

In general, everyone who has physical or mental pain, even animals, understands their own suffering; but when Buddha says 'You should know sufferings' he means that we should know the sufferings of our future lives. Through knowing these, we will develop a strong wish to liberate ourself from them. This practical advice is important for everybody because, if we have the wish to liberate ourself from the sufferings of future lives, we will definitely use our present human life for the freedom and happiness of our countless future lives. There is no greater meaning than this.

If we do not have this wish, we will waste our precious human life only for the freedom and happiness of this one short life. This would be foolish because our intention and actions would be no different from the intention and actions of animals who are only concerned with this life alone. The great Yogi Milarepa once said to a hunter called Gonpo Dorje:

Your body is human but your mind is that of an
   animal.
You, a human being, who possess an animal's mind,
   please listen to my song.

Normally we believe that solving the suffering and problems of our present life is most important, and we dedicate our whole life for this purpose. In reality, the duration of the suffering and problems of this life is very short; if we die tomorrow, they will end tomorrow. However, since the duration of the suffering and problems of future lives is endless, the freedom and happiness of our future lives is vastly more important than the freedom and happiness of this one short life. With the words 'You should know sufferings' Buddha encourages us to use our present human life to prepare for the freedom and happiness of our countless future lives. Those who do this are truly wise.

In future lives, when we are born as an animal, such as a cow or a fish, we will become the food of other living beings, and we will have to experience many other kinds of animal suffering. Animals have no freedom, and are used by human beings for food, work and enjoyment. They have no opportunity to improve themselves; even if they hear precious Dharma words it is as meaningless to them as hearing the wind blowing. When we are born as a hungry ghost we will not have even a tiny drop of water to drink; our only water will be our tears. We will have to experience the unbearable sufferings of thirst and hunger for many hundreds of years. When we are born as a hell being in the hot hells our body will become inseparable from fire, and others will be able to distinguish between our body and fire only by hearing our suffering cries. We will have to experience the unbearable torment of our body being burned for millions of years. Like all other phenomena, the hell realms do not exist inherently but exist as mere appearances to mind, like dreams. When we are born as a desire realm god we experience great conflict and dissatisfaction. Even if we experience some superficial enjoyment, still our desires grow stronger, and we have even more mental suffering than human beings. When we are born as a demi-god we are always jealous of the gods' glory and because of this we have great mental suffering. Our jealousy is like a thorn piercing our mind, causing us to experience both mental and physical suffering for long periods of time. When we are born as a human being we will have to experience various kinds of human suffering, including the sufferings of birth, sickness, ageing and death.

BIRTH

When our consciousness first enters the union of our father's sperm and our mother's ovum, our body is a very hot, watery substance like white yoghurt tinted red. In the first moments after conception we have no gross feelings, but as soon as these develop we begin to experience pain. Our body gradually becomes harder and harder, and as our limbs grow it feels as if our body is being stretched out on a rack. Inside our mother's womb it is hot and dark. Our home for nine months is this small, tightly compressed space full of unclean substances. It is like being squashed inside a small water tank full of filthy liquid with the lid tightly shut so that no air or light can come through.

While we are in our mother's womb we experience much pain and fear all on our own. We are extremely sensitive to everything our mother does. When she walks quickly it feels as if we are falling from a high mountain and we are terrified. If she has sexual intercourse it feels as if we are being crushed and suffocated between two huge weights and we panic. If our mother makes just a small jump it feels as if we are being dashed against the ground from a great height. If she drinks anything hot it feels like boiling water scalding our skin, and if she drinks anything cold it feels like an ice-cold shower in midwinter.

When we are emerging from our mother's womb it feels as if we are being forced through a narrow crevice between two hard rocks, and when we are newly born our body is so delicate that any kind of contact is painful. Even if someone holds us very tenderly, his or her hands feel like thorn bushes piercing our flesh, and the most delicate fabrics feel rough and abrasive. By comparison with the softness and smoothness of our mother's womb, every tactile sensation is harsh and painful. If someone picks us up it feels as if we are being swung over a huge precipice, and we feel frightened and insecure. We have forgotten all that we knew in our previous life; we bring only pain and confusion from our mother's womb. Whatever we hear is as meaningless as the sound of wind, and we cannot comprehend anything we perceive. In the first few weeks we are like someone who is blind, deaf and dumb, and suffering from profound amnesia. When we are hungry we cannot say 'I need food', and when we are in pain we cannot say 'This is hurting me.' The only signs we can make are hot tears and furious gestures. Our mother often has no idea what pains and discomforts we are experiencing. We are completely helpless and have to be taught everything – how to eat, how to sit, how to walk, how to talk.

Although we are most vulnerable in the first few weeks of our life, our pains do not cease as we grow up. We continue to experience various kinds of suffering throughout our life. Just as when we light a fire in a large house, the heat from the fire pervades the whole house and all the heat in the house comes from the fire, so when we are born in samsara, suffering pervades our whole life, and all the miseries we experience arise because we took a contaminated rebirth.

Our human rebirth, contaminated by the poisonous delusion of self-grasping, is the basis of our human suffering; without this basis, there are no human problems. The pains of birth gradually turn into the pains of sickness, ageing and death – they are one continuum.

SICKNESS

Our birth also gives rise to the suffering of sickness. Just as the wind and snow of winter take away the glory of green meadows, trees, forests and flowers, so sickness takes away the youthful splendour of our body, destroying its strength and the power of our senses. If we are usually fit and well, when we become sick we are suddenly unable to engage in all our normal physical activities. Even a champion boxer who is usually able to knock out all his opponents becomes completely helpless when sickness strikes. Sickness makes all our experiences of daily enjoyments disappear and causes us to experience unpleasant feelings day and night.

When we fall ill, we are like a bird that has been soaring in the sky and is suddenly shot down. When a bird is shot, it falls straight to the ground like a lump of lead, and all its glory and power are immediately destroyed. In a similar way, when we become ill we are suddenly incapacitated. If we are seriously ill we may become completely dependent upon others and lose even the ability to control our bodily functions. This transformation is hard to bear, especially for those who pride themselves on their independence and physical well-being.

When we are ill, we feel frustrated as we cannot do our usual work or complete all the tasks we have set ourself. We easily become impatient with our illness and depressed about all the things we cannot do. We cannot enjoy the things that usually give us pleasure, such as sport, dancing, drinking, eating rich foods, or the company of our friends. All these limitations make us feel even more miserable; and, to add to our unhappiness, we have to endure all the physical pains the illness brings.

When we are sick, not only do we have to experience all the unwanted pains of the illness itself, but we also have to experience all sorts of other unwished for things. For example, we have to take whatever cure is prescribed, whether it be a foul-tasting medicine, a series of injections, a major operation, or abstinence from something we like very much. If we are to have an operation, we have to go to hospital and accept all the conditions there. We may have to eat food we do not like and stay in bed all day long with nothing to do, and we may feel anxiety about the operation. Our doctor may not explain to us exactly what the problem is and whether or not he or she expects us to survive.

If we learn that our sickness is incurable, and we have no spiritual experience, we will suffer anxiety, fear and regret.

We may become depressed and give up hope, or we may become angry with our illness, feeling that it is an enemy that has maliciously deprived us of all joy.

AGEING

Our birth also gives rise to the pains of ageing. Ageing steals our beauty, our health, our good figure, our fine complexion, our vitality and our comfort. Ageing turns us into objects of contempt. It brings many unwanted pains and takes us swiftly to our death.

As we grow old we lose all the beauty of our youth, and our strong, healthy body becomes weak and burdened with illness. Our once firm and well-proportioned figure becomes bent and disfigured, and our muscles and flesh shrink so that our limbs become like thin sticks and our bones poke out. Our hair loses its colour and shine, and our complexion loses its lustre. Our face becomes wrinkled and our features grow distorted. Milarepa said:

How do old people get up? They get up as if they were heaving a stake out of the ground. How do old people walk about? Once they are on their feet they have to walk gingerly, like bird-catchers. How do old people sit down? They crash down like heavy luggage whose harness has snapped.

We can contemplate the following poem on the sufferings of growing old, written by the scholar Gungtang:

When we are old, our hair becomes white,
But not because we have washed it clean;
It is a sign we will soon encounter the Lord of Death.

We have wrinkles on our forehead,
But not because we have too much flesh;
It is a warning from the Lord of Death: 'You are about
to die.'

Our teeth fall out,
But not to make room for new ones;
It is a sign we will soon lose the ability to eat human
food.

Our faces are ugly and unpleasant,
But not because we are wearing masks;
It is a sign we have lost the mask of youth.

Our heads shake to and fro,
But not because we are in disagreement;
It is the Lord of Death striking our head with the stick
he holds in his right hand.

We walk bent and gazing at the ground,
But not because we are searching for lost needles;
It is a sign we are searching for our lost beauty and
memories.

We get up from the ground using all four limbs,
But not because we are imitating animals;
It is a sign our legs are too weak to support our body.

We sit down as if we had suddenly fallen,
But not because we are angry;
It is a sign our body has lost its strength.

Our body sways as we walk,
But not because we think we are important;
It is a sign our legs cannot carry our body.

Our hands shake,
But not because they are itching to steal;
It is a sign the Lord of Death's itchy fingers are
    stealing our possessions.

We eat very little,
But not because we are miserly;
It is a sign we cannot digest our food.

We wheeze frequently,
But not because we are whispering mantras to the
    sick;
It is a sign our breathing will soon disappear.

When we are young we can travel around the whole
world, but when we are old we can hardly make it to our own
front gate. We become too weak to engage in many worldly
activities, and our spiritual activities are often curtailed. For
example, we have little physical strength to perform virtuous
actions, and little mental energy to memorize, contemplate
and meditate. We cannot attend teachings that are given in
places that are hard to reach or uncomfortable to inhabit. We
cannot help others in ways that require physical strength
and good health. Deprivations such as these often make old
people very sad.

When we grow old, we become like someone who is blind
and deaf. We cannot see clearly, and we need stronger and
stronger glasses until we can no longer read. We cannot hear
clearly, and so it becomes more and more difficult to listen
to music or to the television, or to hear what others are saying. Our memory fades. All activities, worldly and spiritual,
become more difficult. If we practise meditation it becomes
harder for us to gain realizations because our memory and

concentration are too weak. We cannot apply ourself to study. Thus, if we have not learnt and trained in spiritual practices when we were younger, the only thing to do when we grow old is to develop regret and wait for the Lord of Death to come.

When we are old we cannot derive the same enjoyment from the things we used to enjoy, such as food, drink and sex. We are too weak to play games and we are often too exhausted even for entertainments. As our lifespan runs out we cannot join young people in their activities. When they travel about we have to stay behind. No one wants to take us with them when we are old, and no one wants to visit us. Even our own grandchildren do not want to stay with us for very long. Old people often think to themselves, 'How wonderful it would be if young people would stay with me. We could go out for walks and I could show them things'; but young people do not want to be included in their plans. As their life draws to an end, old people experience the sorrow of abandonment and loneliness. They have many special sorrows.

DEATH

Our birth also gives rise to the sufferings of death. If during our life we have worked hard to acquire possessions, and if we have become very attached to them, we will experience great suffering at the time of death, thinking, 'Now I have to leave all my precious possessions behind.' Even now we find it difficult to lend one of our most treasured possessions to someone else, let alone to give it away. No wonder we become so miserable when we realize that in the hands of death we must abandon everything.

When we die we have to part from even our closest friends. We have to leave our partner, even though we may have been together for years and never spent a day apart. If we are very attached to our friends we will experience great misery at the time of death, but all we will be able to do is hold their hands. We will not be able to halt the process of death, even if they plead with us not to die. Usually when we are very attached to someone we feel jealous if he or she leaves us on our own and spends time with someone else, but when we die we will have to leave our friends with others forever. We will have to leave everyone, including our family and all the people who have helped us in this life.

When we die, this body that we have cherished and cared for in so many ways will have to be left behind. It will become mindless like a stone, and will be buried in the ground or cremated. If we do not have the inner protection of spiritual experience, at the time of death we will experience fear and distress, as well as physical pain.

When our consciousness departs from our body at death, all the potentialities we have accumulated in our mind by performing virtuous and non-virtuous actions will go with it. Other than these we cannot take anything out of this world. All other things deceive us. Death ends all our activities – our conversation, our eating, our meeting with friends, our sleep. Everything draws to a close on the day of our death and we must leave all things behind, even the rings on our fingers. In Tibet beggars carry a stick to defend themselves against dogs. To understand the complete deprivation of death we should remember that at the time of death beggars have to leave even this old stick, the most meagre of human possessions. All over the world we can see that names carved on stone are the only possessions of the dead.

OTHER TYPES OF SUFFERING

We also have to experience the sufferings of separation, having to encounter what we do not like and not fulfilling our wishes – which include the sufferings of poverty, and of being harmed by humans and non-humans and by water, fire, wind and earth. Before the final separation at the time of death we often have to experience temporary separation from the people and things we like, which causes us mental pain. We may have to leave our country where all our friends and relatives live, or we may have to leave the job we like. We may lose our reputation. Many times in this life we have to experience the misery of departing from the people we like, or forsaking and losing the things we find pleasant and attractive; but when we die we have to part forever from all our companions and enjoyments, and from all the outer and inner conditions for our Dharma practice, of this life.

We often have to meet and live with people whom we do not like, or encounter situations that we find unpleasant. Sometimes we may find ourself in a very dangerous situation such as in a fire or a flood, or where there is violence such as in a riot or a battle. Our lives are full of less extreme situations that we find annoying. Sometimes we are prevented from doing the things we want to do. On a sunny day we may set off for the beach but find ourself stuck in a traffic jam. We continually experience interference from our inner demon of delusions, which disturbs our mind and our spiritual practices. There are countless conditions that frustrate our plans and prevent us from doing what we want. It is as if we are naked and living in a thorn bush – whenever we try to move, we are wounded by circumstances. People and things are like thorns piercing our flesh and no situation ever feels entirely comfortable. The more desires and plans we have, the more frustrations we experience. The more we want certain situations, the more we find ourself stuck in situations we do not want. Every desire seems to invite its own obstacle. Undesired situations befall us without our looking for them. In fact, the only things that come effortlessly are the things we do not want. No one wants to die, but death comes effortlessly. No one wants to be sick, but sickness comes effortlessly. Because we have taken rebirth without freedom or control, we have an impure body and inhabit an impure environment, and so undesirable things pour in upon us. In samsara, this kind of experience is entirely natural.

We have countless desires, but no matter how much effort we make we never feel that we have satisfied them. Even when we get what we want, we do not get it in the way we want. We possess the object but we do not derive satisfaction from possessing it. For example, we may dream of becoming wealthy, but if we actually become wealthy our life is not the way we imagined it would be, and we do not feel that we have fulfilled our desire. This is because our desires do not decrease as our wealth increases. The more wealth we have, the more we desire. The wealth we seek is unfindable because we seek an amount that will satiate our desires, and no amount of wealth can do that. To make things worse, in obtaining the object of our desire we create new occasions for discontent. With every object we desire come other objects we do not want. For example, with wealth come taxes, insecurity and complicated financial affairs. These unwished for accessories prevent us from ever feeling fully satisfied. Similarly, we may dream of having a holiday in the South Seas, and we may actually go there on holiday, but the experience is never quite what we expect, and with our holiday come other things such as sunburn and great expense.

If we examine our desires we will see that they are excessive. We want all the best things in samsara – the best job, the best partner, the best reputation, the best house, the best car, the best holiday. Anything that is not the best leaves us with a feeling of disappointment – still searching for but not finding what we want. No worldly enjoyment, however, can give us the complete and perfect satisfaction we desire. Better things are always being produced. Everywhere, new advertisements announce that the very best thing has just arrived on the market, but a few days later another best thing arrives that is better than the best thing of a few days ago. There is no end of new things to captivate our desires.

Children at school can never satisfy their own or their parents' ambitions. Even if they come top of their class they feel they cannot be content unless they do the same the following year. If they go on to be successful in their jobs, their ambitions will be as strong as ever. There is no point at which they can rest, feeling that they are completely satisfied with what they have done.

We may think that at least people who lead a simple life in the country must be content, but if we look at their situation we will find that even farmers search for but do not find what they want. Their lives are full of problems and anxieties, and they do not enjoy real peace and satisfaction. Their livelihoods depend upon many uncertain factors beyond their control, such as the weather. Farmers have no more freedom from discontent than businessmen who live and work in the city. Businessmen look smart and efficient as they set off to work each morning carrying their briefcases but, although they look so smooth on the outside, in their hearts they carry many dissatisfactions. They are still searching for but not finding what they want.

If we reflect on this situation we may decide that we can find what we are searching for by abandoning all our possessions. We can see, however, that even poor people are looking for but not finding what they seek, and many poor people have difficulty in finding even the most basic necessities of life; millions of people in the world experience the sufferings of extreme poverty.

We cannot avoid the suffering of dissatisfaction by frequently changing our situation. We may think that if we keep getting a new partner or a new job, or keep travelling about, we will eventually find what we want; but even if we were to travel to every place on the globe, and have a new lover in every town, we would still be seeking another place and another lover. In samsara there is no real fulfilment of our desires.

Whenever we see anyone in a high or low position, male or female, they differ only in appearance, dress, behaviour and status. In essence they are all equal – they all experience problems in their lives. Whenever we have a problem, it is easy to think that it is caused by our particular circumstances, and that if we were to change our circumstances our problem would disappear. We blame other people, our friends, our food, our government, our times, the weather, society, history and so forth. However, external circumstances such as these are not the main causes of our problems. We need to recognize that all the physical suffering and mental pain we experience are the consequences of our taking a rebirth that is contaminated by the inner poison of delusions. Human beings have to experience various kinds of human suffering because they have taken a contaminated human rebirth; animals have to experience animal suffering because they have taken a contaminated animal rebirth; and hungry ghosts and hell beings have to experience their own sufferings because they have taken contaminated rebirth as hungry ghosts and hell beings. Even gods are not free from suffering because they too have taken a contaminated rebirth. Just as a person trapped inside a raging fire develops intense fear, so we should develop intense fear of the unbearable sufferings of the endless cycle of impure life. This fear is real renunciation and arises from our wisdom.

In conclusion, having contemplated the above explanation we should think:

There is no benefit in denying the sufferings of future lives; when they actually descend upon me it will be too late to protect myself from them. Therefore I definitely need to prepare protection now, while I have this human life that gives me the opportunity to liberate myself permanently from the sufferings of my countless future lives. If I do not apply effort to accomplish this, but allow my human life to become empty of meaning, there is no greater deception and no greater foolishness. I must put effort now into liberating myself permanently from the sufferings of my countless future lives.

We meditate on this determination continually until we develop the spontaneous wish to liberate ourself permanently from the sufferings of countless future lives. This is the actual realization of renunciation. The moment we develop this realization we enter the path to liberation. In this context, liberation refers to the supreme permanent peace of mind known as 'nirvana', which gives us pure and everlasting happiness.

WHAT WE SHOULD ABANDON

In *Sutra of the Four Noble Truths* Buddha says, 'You should abandon origins.' In saying this Buddha is advising us that if we wish to liberate ourself permanently from the sufferings of our countless future lives we should abandon origins. 'Origins' means our delusions, principally our delusion of self-grasping. Self-grasping is called an 'origin' because it is the source of all our suffering and problems, and is also known as the 'inner demon'. Delusions are wrong awarenesses whose function is to destroy mental peace, the source of happiness; they have no function other than to harm us. Delusions such as self-grasping abide at our heart and continually harm us day and night without rest by destroying our peace of mind. In samsara, the cycle of impure life, no one has the opportunity to experience real happiness because their mental peace, the source of happiness, is continually being destroyed by the inner demon of self-grasping.

Our self-grasping ignorance is a mind that mistakenly believes that our self, our body and all the other things that we normally see actually exist. Because of this ignorance we develop attachment to the things we like and anger at the things we do not like. We then perform various kinds of non-virtuous action, and as a result of these actions we experience various kinds of suffering and problems in this life and in life after life.

Self-grasping ignorance is an inner poison that causes far greater harm than any outer poison. Because of being polluted by this inner poison, our mind sees everything in a mistaken way, and as a result we experience hallucination-like sufferings and problems. In reality, our self, our body and all the other things that we normally see do not exist. Self-grasping can be likened to a poisonous tree, all other delusions to its branches, and all our suffering and problems to its fruit; it is the fundamental source of all our other delusions and of all our suffering and problems. Through this we can understand that if we abandon our self-grasping permanently, all our suffering and problems of this life and of countless future lives will cease permanently. The great Yogi Saraha said, 'If your mind is released permanently from self-grasping, there is no doubt that you will be released permanently from suffering.' Understanding this and having contemplated the above explanations, we should think:

> I must apply great effort to recognizing, reducing and finally abandoning my ignorance of self-grasping completely.

We should meditate on this determination continually, and put our determination into practice.

WHAT WE SHOULD PRACTISE

In *Sutra of the Four Noble Truths* Buddha says, 'You should practise the path.' In this context, 'path' does not mean an external path that leads from one place to another, but an inner path, a spiritual realization that leads us to the pure happiness of liberation and enlightenment.

The practice of the stages of the path to liberation can be condensed into the three trainings of higher moral discipline, higher concentration and higher wisdom. These trainings are called 'higher' because they are motivated by renunciation. They are therefore the actual path to liberation that we need to practise.

The nature of moral discipline is a virtuous determination to abandon inappropriate actions. When we practise moral discipline we abandon inappropriate actions, maintain pure behaviour and perform every action correctly with a virtuous motivation. Moral discipline is most important for everybody in order to prevent future problems for ourself and for others. It makes us pure because it makes our actions pure. We need to be clean and pure ourself; just having a clean body is not enough, since our body is not our self. Moral discipline is like a great earth that supports and nurtures the crops of spiritual realizations. Without practising moral discipline, it is very difficult to make progress in spiritual training. Training in higher moral discipline is learning to be deeply familiar with the practice of moral discipline, motivated by renunciation.

The second higher training is training in higher concentration. The nature of concentration is a single-pointed virtuous mind. For as long as we remain with this mind we will experience mental peace, and thus we will be happy. When we practise concentration we prevent distractions and concentrate on virtuous objects. It is very important to train in concentration, as with distractions we cannot accomplish anything. Training in higher concentration is learning to be deeply familiar with the ability to stop distractions and concentrate on virtuous objects, with a motivation of renunciation. With regard to any Dharma practice, if our concentration is clear and strong it is very easy to make progress. Normally, distraction is the main obstacle to our Dharma practice. The practice of moral discipline prevents gross distractions, and concentration prevents subtle distractions; together they give rise to quick results in our Dharma practice.

The third higher training is training in higher wisdom. The nature of wisdom is a virtuous intelligent mind that functions to understand meaningful objects such as the existence of past and future lives, karma and emptiness. Understanding these objects brings great meaning to this life and countless future lives. Many people are very intelligent in destroying their enemies, caring for their families, finding what they want and so forth, but this is not wisdom. Even animals have such intelligence. Worldly intelligence is deceptive, whereas wisdom will never deceive us. It is our inner Spiritual Guide who leads us to correct paths, and it is the divine eye through which we can see past and future lives, and the special connection between our actions in past lives and our experiences in this life, known as 'karma'. The subject of karma is very extensive and subtle, and we can understand it only through wisdom. Training in higher wisdom is learning to develop and increase our wisdom realizing emptiness through contemplating and meditating on emptiness, with a motivation of renunciation. This wisdom is extremely profound. Its object, emptiness, is not nothingness but is the real nature of all phenomena. A detailed explanation of emptiness has been given in Part One.

The three higher trainings are the actual method to attain permanent liberation from the suffering of this life and countless future lives. This can be understood by the following analogy. When we cut down a tree using a saw, the saw alone cannot cut the tree without the use of our hands, which in turn depend upon our body. Training in higher moral discipline is like our body, training in higher concentration is like our hands, and training in higher wisdom is like the saw. By using these three together, we can cut down the poisonous tree of our self-grasping ignorance, and automatically all other delusions – its branches – and all our suffering and problems – its fruits – will cease completely. Then we will have attained the permanent cessation of the suffering of this life and future lives – the supreme permanent peace of mind known as 'nirvana', or liberation. We will have solved all our human problems and accomplished the real meaning of our life.

Contemplating the above explanation we should think:

Since the three higher trainings are the actual method to attain permanent liberation from the suffering of this life and countless future lives, I must put great effort into practising them.

We should meditate on this determination continually, and put our determination into practice.

WHAT WE SHOULD ATTAIN

In *Sutra of the Four Noble Truths* Buddha says, 'You should attain cessations.' In this context, 'cessation' means the permanent cessation of suffering and its root, self-grasping ignorance. In saying this, Buddha is advising us not to be satisfied with a temporary liberation from particular sufferings, but that we should have the intention to accomplish the ultimate goal of human life, the supreme permanent peace of mind (nirvana), and the pure and everlasting happiness of enlightenment.

Every living being without exception has to experience the cycle of the sufferings of sickness, ageing, death and rebirth, in life after life, endlessly. Following Buddha's example, we should develop strong renunciation for this endless cycle. When he was living in the palace with his family, Buddha saw how his people were constantly experiencing these sufferings and he made the strong determination to attain enlightenment, great liberation, and to lead every living being to this state.

Buddha did not encourage us to abandon daily activities that provide necessary conditions for living, or that prevent poverty, environmental problems, particular diseases and so forth. However, no matter how successful we are in these activities, we will never achieve permanent cessation of such problems. We will still have to experience them in our countless future lives and, even in this life, although we work very hard to prevent these problems, the sufferings of poverty, environmental pollution and disease are increasing throughout the world. Furthermore, because of the power of modern technology there are now many great dangers developing in the world that have never been experienced before. Therefore, we should not be satisfied with merely temporary freedom from particular sufferings, but apply great effort to attaining permanent freedom while we have this opportunity.

We should remember the preciousness of our human life. Because of their previous deluded views denying the value of spiritual practice, those who have taken rebirth as animals, for example, have no opportunity to engage in spiritual practice, which alone gives rise to a meaningful life. Since it is impossible for them to listen to, understand, contemplate and meditate on spiritual instructions, their present animal rebirth itself is an obstacle. As mentioned earlier, only human beings are free from such obstacles and have all the necessary conditions for engaging in spiritual paths, which alone lead to everlasting peace and happiness. This combination of freedom and the possession of necessary conditions is the special characteristic that makes our human life so precious. In conclusion, we should think:

I should not be satisfied with a merely temporary cessation of particular sufferings, which even animals can experience. I must attain the permanent cessation of self-grasping ignorance – the root of suffering – through sincerely practising the three higher trainings.

We should meditate on this determination every day, and put our determination into practice. In this way we guide ourself to the liberating path.

Je Phabongkhapa

The Path of a Person of Great Scope

In this context, a 'person of great scope' refers to someone who has a great capacity for developing spiritual understanding and realizations.

Because this subject is extensive, a detailed explanation of it will be given in the following chapters.

The Supreme Good Heart – Bodhichitta

We should maintain renunciation – the sincere wish to attain permanent liberation – day and night. It is the door to liberation – the supreme permanent peace of mind – and the basis of more advanced realizations. However, we should not be content with seeking merely our own liberation; we need also to consider the welfare of other living beings. There are countless beings drowning in samsara's ocean experiencing unbearable suffering. Whereas each one of us is just one single person, other living beings are countless in number; therefore the happiness and freedom of others are much more important than our own. For this reason we must enter the Bodhisattva's path, which leads us to the state of full enlightenment.

The gateway through which we enter the Bodhisattva's path is bodhichitta. 'Bodhi' means enlightenment and 'chitta' means mind. Bodhichitta is a mind that spontaneously wishes to attain enlightenment to benefit each and every living being directly. The moment we develop this precious mind of bodhichitta we become a Bodhisattva – a person who spontaneously wishes to attain enlightenment for the benefit of all living beings – and we become a Son or Daughter of the Conqueror Buddhas.

This supreme good heart of bodhichitta cannot be developed without training. Je Tsongkhapa said:

Through watering the ground of affectionate love with
    cherishing love,
And then sowing the seeds of wishing love and
    compassion,
The medicinal tree of bodhichitta will grow.

This implies that there are five stages of training in bodhichitta:

1 Training in affectionate love
2 Training in cherishing love
3 Training in wishing love
4 Training in universal compassion
5 Training in actual bodhichitta

TRAINING IN AFFECTIONATE LOVE

In this training we learn to develop and maintain a warm heart and a feeling of being close to all living beings without exception. This affectionate love makes our mind pure and balanced, and prepares the foundation for generating cherishing love for all living beings. Normally our mind is unbalanced; we feel either too close to someone out of attachment or too distant from others out of anger. It is impossible to develop the supreme good heart of bodhichitta with such an unbalanced mind. This unbalanced mind is the source of all our daily problems. We may think that some people are our enemies because they are harming us, so how can we develop and maintain a warm heart and a feeling of being close to such people? This way of thinking is incorrect. The people who we believe are our enemies are in reality our mothers of former lives. Our mothers of former lives and our mother of this present life are all our mothers and are all equally kind to us.

It is incorrect to reason that our mothers of former lives are no longer our mothers just because a long time has passed since they actually cared for us. If our present mother were to die today, would she cease to be our mother? No, we would still regard her as our mother and pray for her happiness. The same is true of all our previous mothers – they died, yet they remain our mothers. It is only because of the changes in our external appearance that we do not recognize each other.

In our daily life, we see many different living beings, both human and non-human. We regard some as friends, some as enemies, and most as strangers. These distinctions are made by our mistaken minds; they are not verified by valid minds. Rather than following such mistaken minds, we should recognize and believe that all living beings are our mothers. Whoever we meet, we should think, 'This person is my mother.' In this way, we will generate a warm heart and a feeling of being equally close to all living beings. Our belief that all living beings are our mothers is wisdom because it understands a meaningful object, which is that all living beings are our mothers. Through this understanding we will experience great meaning in this life and in countless future lives. We should never abandon this beneficial belief or view.

We should contemplate as follows:

Since it is impossible to find a beginning to my mental continuum, it follows that I have taken countless rebirths in the past, and, if I have had countless rebirths, I must have had countless mothers. Where are all these mothers now? They are all the living beings alive today.

Having repeatedly contemplated this point we strongly believe that all living beings are our mothers, and we meditate on this belief.

THE KINDNESS OF LIVING BEINGS

Having become convinced that all living beings are our mothers, we contemplate the immense kindness we have received from each of them when they were our mother, as well as the kindness they have shown us at other times.

When we were conceived, had our mother not wanted to keep us in her womb she could have had an abortion. If she had done so, we would not now have this human life. Through her kindness she allowed us to stay in her womb, and so we now enjoy a human life and experience all its advantages. When we were a baby, had we not received her constant care and attention we would certainly have had an accident and could now be disabled or blind. Fortunately, our mother did not neglect us. Day and night, she gave us her loving care, regarding us as more important than herself. She saved our life many times each day. During the night she allowed her sleep to be interrupted, and during the day she forfeited her usual pleasures. She had to leave her job, and when her friends went out to enjoy themselves she had to stay behind. She spent all her money on us, giving us the best food and the best clothes she could afford. She taught us how to eat, how to walk, how to talk. Thinking of our future welfare, she did her best to ensure that we received a good education. Due to her kindness, we are now able to study whatever we choose. It is principally through the kindness of our mother that we now have the opportunity to practise Dharma and eventually to attain enlightenment.

Since there is no one who has not been our mother at some time in our previous lives, and since when we were their child they treated us with the same kindness as our present mother has treated us in this life, all living beings are very kind.

The kindness of living beings is not limited to the times when they have been our mother. All the time, our day-to-day needs are provided through the kindness of others. We brought nothing with us from our former life, yet, as soon as we were born, we were given a home, food, clothes, and everything we needed – all provided through the kindness of others. Everything we now enjoy has been provided through the kindness of other beings, past or present.

We are able to make use of many things with very little effort on our own part. If we consider facilities such as roads, cars, trains, aeroplanes, ships, houses, restaurants, hotels, libraries, hospitals, shops, money and so on, it is clear that many people worked very hard to provide these things. Even though we make little or no contribution towards the provision of these facilities, they are all available for us to use. This shows the great kindness of others.

Both our general education and our spiritual training are provided by others. All our Dharma realizations, from our very first insights up to our eventual attainment of liberation and enlightenment, will be attained in dependence upon the kindness of others. As human beings we generally have the opportunity to attain the supreme happiness of enlightenment. This is because we have the opportunity to enter and follow the path to enlightenment, a spiritual path motivated by compassion for all living beings. The gateway through which we enter the path to enlightenment is therefore compassion for all living beings – universal compassion – and we develop this compassion only by relying upon all living beings as the objects of our compassion. This shows that it is through the great kindness of all living beings acting as the objects of our compassion that we have the opportunity to enter the path to enlightenment and attain the supreme happiness of enlightenment. It is therefore clear that for us all living beings are supremely kind and precious.

From the depths of our heart we should think:

Each and every living being is supremely kind and precious to me. They provide me with the opportunity to attain the pure and everlasting happiness of enlightenment – the ultimate goal of human life.

Understanding and thinking in this way, we generate a warm heart and a feeling of being equally close to all living beings without exception. We transform our mind into this feeling, and we remain on it single-pointedly for as long as possible. Through continually contemplating and meditating in this way we will maintain a warm heart and a feeling of being close to each and every living being all the time, in every situation. Having understood the eight benefits of maintaining affectionate love that are listed below in the section *Wishing Love*, we should apply continual effort in this practice.

TRAINING IN CHERISHING LOVE

This training has two stages:

1 Equalizing self and others
2 Exchanging self with others

EQUALIZING SELF AND OTHERS

This practice is called 'equalizing self and others' because we are learning to believe that the happiness and freedom of ourself and all other living beings are equally important. Learning to cherish others is the best solution to our daily problems, and it is the source of all our future happiness and good fortune.

There are two levels of cherishing others: (1) cherishing others as we cherish a close friend or relative; and (2) cherishing others as we cherish ourself. The second level is more profound. Through cherishing all living beings as we cherish ourself we will develop the profound universal compassion that functions as the quick path to enlightenment. This is one of the essential points of Kadam Lamrim.

To train in equalizing self and others we engage in the following contemplation, thinking:

I must believe that the happiness and freedom of myself and all other living beings are equally important because:

(1) All living beings have shown me great kindness in both this and previous lives.

(2) Just as I wish to be free from suffering and experience only happiness, so do all other beings. In this respect, I am no different from any other being; we are all equal.

(3) I am only one, whereas others are countless, so how can I be concerned for myself alone while I neglect others? My happiness and suffering are insignificant when compared with the happiness and suffering of countless other living beings.

Having repeatedly contemplated these points, we strongly believe that the happiness and freedom of ourself and all other living beings are equally important. We then remain on this belief single-pointedly for as long as possible. We should continually practise this contemplation and meditation until we spontaneously believe that the happiness and freedom of ourself and all other living beings are equally important, which is the realization of equalizing self and others.

EXCHANGING SELF WITH OTHERS

This training has three stages:

1 Contemplating the disadvantages of self-cherishing
2 Contemplating the advantages of cherishing others
3 The actual training in exchanging self with others

CONTEMPLATING THE DISADVANTAGES OF SELF-CHERISHING

What exactly is self-cherishing? Self-cherishing is our mind that thinks 'I am important' while neglecting others. When we think 'I' and 'mine' we perceive an inherently existent I, and we cherish it and believe that its happiness and freedom are the most important. This is self-cherishing. Caring for ourself is not self-cherishing. We need to care for ourself to maintain this human life so that we can continually apply effort to accomplishing its real meaning.

Self-cherishing and self-grasping are different aspects of one mind. Self-grasping grasps at an inherently existent 'I', and self-cherishing believes that such an 'I' is precious and that its happiness and freedom are supremely important. Self-cherishing is our normal view that believes 'I am important' and 'My happiness and freedom are important', and that neglects others' happiness and freedom. It is part of our ignorance because in reality there is no inherently exist-ent I. Our self-cherishing mind nevertheless cherishes this I and believes it to be the most important. It is a foolish and deceptive mind that always interferes with our inner peace, and it is a great obstacle to our accomplishing the real mean-ing of our human life. We have had this self-cherishing mind in life after life since beginningless time, even while asleep and dreaming.

In *Guide to the Bodhisattva's Way of Life* Shantideva says:

… all the suffering there is in this world
Arises from wishing ourself to be happy.

Sufferings are not given to us as a punishment. They all come from our self-cherishing mind, which wishes ourself to be happy while neglecting the happiness of others. There are two ways to understand this. First, the self-cherishing mind is the creator of all our suffering and problems; and second, self-cherishing is the basis for experiencing all our suffering and problems.

We suffer because in our previous lives we performed actions that caused others to experience suffering, motiv-ated by selfish intention – our self-cherishing. As a result of these actions, we now experience our present suffering and problems. Therefore, the real creator of all our suffering and problems is our self-cherishing mind.

Our present experience of particular suffering and problems has a special connection with particular actions we performed in our previous lives. This is very subtle. We cannot see this hidden connection with our eyes, but as already explained we can understand it through using our wisdom, and in particular through relying upon Buddha's teachings on karma. In general, everyone knows that if they perform bad actions they will experience bad results and if they perform good actions they will experience good results.

The self-cherishing mind is also the basis for experiencing all our suffering and problems. For example, when people are unable to fulfil their wishes, many experience depression, discouragement, unhappiness and mental pain, and some even want to kill themselves. This is because their self-cherishing believes that their own wishes are so important. It is therefore their self-cherishing that is mainly responsible for their problems. Without self-cherishing, there would be no basis for experiencing such suffering.

When we are seriously ill we find it difficult to bear our suffering, but illness harms us only because we cherish ourself. If another person is experiencing a similar illness, we have no problem. Why? Because we do not cherish him or her. However, if we cherished others as we cherish ourself, we would find it difficult to bear their suffering. This is compassion. As Shantideva says:

> The suffering I experience
> Does not harm others,
> But I find it hard to bear
> Because I cherish myself.
>
> Likewise, the suffering of others
> Does not harm me,
> But, if I cherish others,
> I will find their suffering hard to bear.

In life after life, since beginningless time, we have tried to fulfil the wishes of our self-cherishing mind, believing its view to be true. We have put great effort into seeking happiness from external sources, but have nothing to show for it now. Because self-cherishing has deceived us we have wasted countless previous lives. It has driven us to work for our own purpose, but we have gained nothing. This foolish mind has made all our previous lives empty – when we took this human rebirth we brought nothing with us but delusions. In every moment of every day, this self-cherishing mind continues to deceive us.

Having contemplated these points, we think:

Nothing causes me greater harm than the demon of my self-cherishing. It is the source of all my negativity, misfortune, problems and suffering. Therefore I must abandon my self-cherishing.

We should meditate on this determination every day, and put our determination into practice.

CONTEMPLATING THE ADVANTAGES OF CHERISHING OTHERS

When we deeply think that others are important, and that their happiness and freedom are important, we are cherishing others. If we cherish others like this, we will always have good relationships and live in harmony with others, and our daily life will be peaceful and happy. We can begin this practice with our family, friends and those around us, and then gradually we will develop and maintain cherishing love for all living beings without exception.

In *Guide to the Bodhisattva's Way of Life*, Shantideva says:

All the happiness there is in this world
Arises from wishing others to be happy, ...

If we think carefully about this, we will realize that all our present and future happiness depends upon our cherishing others – upon our wanting others to be happy. In our past lives, because we cherished others, we practised virtuous actions such as refraining from killing or harming others and abandoning stealing from and cheating them. We gave them material help and protection, and practised patience. As a result of these virtuous actions, we have now obtained this precious human life with the opportunity to experience human enjoyments.

The immediate effect of cherishing others will be that many of our daily problems, such as those that arise from anger, jealousy and selfish behaviour, will disappear, and our mind will become calm and peaceful. Since we will act in considerate ways, we will please others and not become involved in quarrels or disputes. If we cherish others we will be concerned to help rather than to harm them, so we will naturally avoid non-virtuous actions. Instead, we will practise virtuous actions, such as compassion, love, patience, and giving material help and protection, and thus create the cause to attain pure and everlasting happiness in the future.

In particular, if we cherish all other living beings as we cherish ourself we will find their suffering hard to bear. Our feeling that it is hard to bear the suffering of all other living beings is universal compassion, and this will lead us quickly to the pure and everlasting happiness of enlightenment. Just like all the previous Buddhas, we will be born an enlightened Buddha from the mother, universal compassion. This is why our cherishing all living beings will enable us to attain enlightenment very quickly.

Contemplating all these benefits, we think:

The precious mind that cherishes all living beings protects both myself and others from suffering, brings pure and everlasting happiness and fulfils the wishes of both myself and others. Therefore I must always cherish all living beings without exception.

We should meditate on this determination every day, and out of meditation put our determination into practice. This means that we should actually cherish each and every living being, including animals.

THE ACTUAL TRAINING IN EXCHANGING SELF WITH OTHERS

Exchanging self with others means that we change the object of our cherishing from ourself to all other living beings. This is impossible without training. How do we train in exchanging self with others? With an understanding of the great disadvantages of cherishing ourself and the great advantages of cherishing all living beings, as explained above, and remembering that we have made the determination to abandon our self-cherishing and always cherish all living beings without exception, we think from the depths of our heart:

I must give up cherishing myself and instead cherish all other living beings without exception.

We then meditate on this determination. We should continually practise this meditation until we spontaneously believe that the happiness and freedom of each and every other living being are far more important than our own. This belief is the realization of exchanging self with others.

TRAINING IN WISHING LOVE

With the understanding and belief that the happiness and freedom of each and every living being are far more important than our own, we generate wishing love for all living beings, thinking:

How wonderful it would be if all living beings attained the pure and everlasting happiness of enlightenment! May they attain this happiness. I myself will work for this aim.

We remain single-pointedly on this precious mind of wishing love for all living beings for as long as possible. We repeat this meditation again and again until we spontaneously wish that each and every living being may experience the happiness of enlightenment. This spontaneous wish is the actual realization of wishing love.

Wishing love is also called 'immeasurable love' because merely through meditating on wishing love we will receive immeasurable benefits in this life and in countless future lives. Based on Buddha's teachings, the great scholar Nagarjuna listed eight benefits of affectionate love and wishing love: (1) By meditating on affectionate love and wishing love for just one moment we accumulate greater merit than we would do by giving food three times every day to all those who are hungry in the world.

When we give food to those who are hungry we are not giving real happiness. This is because the happiness that comes from eating food is not real happiness, but just a temporary reduction in the suffering of hunger. However, meditation on affectionate love and wishing love leads us and all living beings to the pure and everlasting happiness of enlightenment.

The remaining seven benefits of meditating on affectionate love and wishing love are that in the future: (2) we will receive great loving kindness from humans and non-humans; (3) we will be protected in various ways by humans and non-humans; (4) we will be mentally happy all the time; (5) we will be physically healthy all the time; (6) we will not be harmed by weapons, poison and other harmful conditions; (7) we will obtain all necessary conditions without effort; and (8) we will be born in the superior heaven of a Buddha Land.

Having contemplated these benefits we should apply effort in meditating on wishing love many times every day.

TRAINING IN UNIVERSAL COMPASSION

Universal compassion is a mind that sincerely wishes to liberate all living beings from suffering permanently. If, on the basis of cherishing all living beings, we contemplate the fact that they experience the cycle of physical suffering and mental pain in life after life without end, their inability to liberate themselves from suffering, their lack of freedom and how, by engaging in negative actions, they create the causes of future suffering, we will develop deep compassion for them. We need to empathize with them and feel their pain as keenly as we feel our own.

No one wants to suffer, yet out of ignorance living beings create suffering by performing non-virtuous actions. We should therefore feel equal compassion for all living beings without exception; there is no single living being who is not a suitable object of our compassion.

All living beings suffer because they take contaminated rebirths. Human beings have no choice but to experience immense human sufferings because they have taken human rebirth, which is contaminated by the inner poison of delusions. Similarly, animals have to experience animal suffering, and hungry ghosts and hell beings have to experience all the sufferings of their respective realms. If living beings were to experience all this suffering for just one single life, it would not be so bad, but the cycle of suffering continues life after life, endlessly.

To develop renunciation, we previously contemplated how in our countless future lives we will have to experience the unbearable sufferings of animals, hungry ghosts, hell beings, humans, demi-gods and gods. Now, at this point, to develop compassion for all living beings who are our mothers, we contemplate how in their countless future lives they will have to experience the unbearable sufferings of animals, hungry ghosts, hell beings, humans, demi-gods and gods.

Having contemplated this we should think:

I cannot bear the suffering of these countless mother beings. Drowning in the vast and deep ocean of samsara, the cycle of contaminated rebirth, they have to experience unbearable physical suffering and mental pain in this life and in countless future lives. I must permanently liberate all these living beings from their suffering.

We should meditate continually on this determination, which is universal compassion, and apply great effort to fulfilling its aim.

TRAINING IN ACTUAL BODHICHITTA

The moment we develop bodhichitta we become a Bodhisattva, a person who spontaneously wishes to attain enlightenment for the benefit of all living beings. Initially we will be a Bodhisattva on the path of accumulation. Then, by following the path to enlightenment with the vehicle of bodhichitta, we can progress from being a Bodhisattva on the path of accumulation to being a Bodhisattva on the path of preparation, a Bodhisattva on the path of seeing, and then a Bodhisattva on the path of meditation. From there we will reach the Path of No More Learning, which is the actual state of enlightenment. As already mentioned, enlightenment is the inner light of wisdom that is permanently free from all mistaken appearance, and whose function is to bestow mental peace upon each and every living being every day. When we attain a Buddha's enlightenment we will be able to benefit each and every living being directly through bestowing blessings and through our countless emanations.

In Sutra teachings, Buddha says:

In this impure life of samsara
No one experiences real happiness;
The actions they perform
Will always be the causes of suffering.

The happiness that we normally experience through having good conditions, such as a good reputation, a good position, a good job, good relationships, seeing attractive forms, hearing good news or beautiful music, eating, drinking and sex is not real happiness, but changing suffering – a reduction in our previous suffering. Out of ignorance, however, we believe that only these things bring happiness, and because of this we never wish to attain real happiness, the pure and everlasting happiness of liberation and enlightenment, even for our own benefit. We are always searching for happiness in this impure life of samsara, like the thief who searched for gold in Milarepa's empty cave and found nothing. The great Yogi Milarepa heard a thief rummaging around his cave one night and called out to him, 'How do you expect to find anything valuable here at night, when I cannot find anything valuable here during the day?'

When, through training, we develop the precious mind of enlightenment, bodhichitta, we spontaneously think:

How wonderful it would be if I and all living beings attained real happiness, the pure and everlasting happiness of enlightenment! May we attain this happiness. I myself will work for this aim.

We need to have this precious mind of bodhichitta in our heart. It is our inner Spiritual Guide, who leads us directly to the state of supreme happiness of enlightenment; and it is the real wishfulfilling jewel through which we can fulfil our own and others' wishes. There is no greater beneficial intention than this precious mind.

Having contemplated the above explanation, we think from the depths of our heart:

I am one single person but other living beings are countless, and they are all my kind mothers. These countless mother beings have to experience unbearable physical suffering and mental pain in this life and in their countless future lives. Compared with the suffering of these countless living beings, my own suffering is insignificant. I must liberate all living beings from suffering permanently, and for this purpose I must attain a Buddha's enlightenment.

We meditate on this determination, which is bodhichitta, single-pointedly. We should practise this contemplation and meditation continually until we develop the spontaneous wish to attain enlightenment to benefit each and every living being directly, and then we should apply great effort to fulfilling our bodhichitta wish.

Dorjechang Trijang Rinpoche

Training in the Path of Bodhichitta

There are three stages of training in the path of bodhichitta:

1 Training in the six perfections
2 Training in taking in conjunction with the practice of the six perfections
3 Training in giving in conjunction with the practice of the six perfections

TRAINING IN THE SIX PERFECTIONS

The six perfections are the actual path to enlightenment, and they are also the path of bodhichitta and the Bodhisattva's path. Through following this path with the vehicle of bodhichitta we will definitely reach the state of enlightenment. Our bodhichitta wish is to attain enlightenment to benefit each and every living being directly. To fulfil this wish, in front of our Spiritual Guide or an image of Buddha regarded as the living Buddha, we should promise to engage in the Bodhisattva's path or training while reciting the following ritual prayer three times. This promise is the Bodhisattva's vow.

Just as all the previous Sugatas, the Buddhas,
Generated the mind of enlightenment, bodhichitta,
And accomplished all the stages
Of the Bodhisattva's training,

So will I too, for the sake of all beings,
Generate the mind of enlightenment
And accomplish all the stages
Of the Bodhisattva's training.

When we take the Bodhisattva's vow we are taking the commitment to engage in the path to enlightenment, the Bodhisattva's training, which is the practice of the six perfections. Normally, when we start a job, we commit ourself to fulfilling our employer's wishes; otherwise we will quickly lose our job. In the same way, having generated bodhichitta – the determination to attain enlightenment to benefit each and every living being directly – we need to commit ourself to engaging in the practice of the six perfections. If we do not make this commitment by taking the Bodhisattva's vow, we will lose our opportunity to attain enlightenment. Through contemplating this we should encourage ourself to take the Bodhisattva's vow and sincerely practise the six perfections.

The six perfections are the practices of giving, moral discipline, patience, effort, concentration and wisdom, motivated by bodhichitta. We should recognize that the six perfections are our daily practice.

In the practice of giving we should practise: (1) giving material help to those in poverty, including giving food to animals; (2) giving practical help to those sick or physically weak; (3) giving protection by always trying to save others' lives, including those of insects; (4) giving love – learning to cherish all living beings by always believing that their happiness and freedom are important; and (5) giving Dharma, helping others to solve their problems of anger, attachment and ignorance by giving Dharma teachings or meaningful advice.

In the practice of moral discipline we should abandon any inappropriate actions including those that cause others suffering. We should especially abandon breaking our commitments of the Bodhisattva's vow. This is the basic foundation upon which we can make progress on the Bodhisattva's path. By doing this our actions of body, speech and mind will be pure, so that we become a pure being.

In the practice of patience we should never allow ourself to become angry or discouraged, by temporarily accepting any difficulties or harm from others. When we practise patience we are wearing the supreme inner armour that directly protects us from physical sufferings, mental pain and other problems. Anger destroys our merit, or good fortune, so that we will continually experience many obstacles, and because of lacking good fortune it will be difficult to fulfil our wishes, especially our spiritual aims. There is no greater evil than anger. With the practice of patience we can accomplish any spiritual aim; there is no greater virtue than patience.

In the practice of effort we should rely upon irreversible effort to accumulate the great collections of merit and wisdom, which are the main causes of attaining Buddha's Form Body (Rupakaya), and Truth Body (Dharmakaya); and especially we should emphasize contemplation and meditation on emptiness, the way things really are. By doing this we can easily make progress on the path to enlightenment. With effort we can accomplish our aim, whereas with laziness we cannot achieve anything.

In the practice of concentration, at this stage we should emphasize accomplishing the concentration of tranquil abiding observing emptiness. An explanation is given in *Modern Buddhism* in the section *A Simple Training in Ultimate Bodhichitta*. When, through the power of this concentration, we experience a special wisdom called 'superior seeing' that realizes the emptiness of all phenomena very clearly, we will have progressed from being a Bodhisattva on the path of accumulation to being a Bodhisattva on the path of preparation.

In the practice of wisdom, at this stage we need to emphasize increasing the power of our wisdom of superior seeing by continually meditating on the emptiness of all phenomena with bodhichitta motivation. Through this, when our superior seeing transforms into the path of seeing, which is the direct realization of the emptiness of all phenomena, we will have progressed from being a Bodhisattva on the path of preparation to being a Bodhisattva on the path of seeing. The moment we attain the path of seeing we are a Superior Bodhisattva and no longer experience samsara's sufferings. As mentioned previously, even if someone cuts our body piece by piece with a knife we have no pain because we have the direct realization of the way things really are.

Having completed the path of seeing, to make further progress we need to engage continually in the meditation on the emptiness of all phenomena with bodhichitta motivation. This meditation is called the 'path of meditation'. When we reach this stage we will have progressed from being a Bodhisattva on the path of seeing to being a Bodhisattva on the path of meditation.

Having completed the path of meditation, when our wisdom of the path of meditation transforms into an omniscient wisdom that is permanently free from all mistaken appearances, this omniscient wisdom is called the 'Path of No More Learning', which is actual enlightenment. When we reach this stage we will have progressed from being a Bodhisattva on the path of meditation to being an enlightened being, a

Buddha. We will have completed the ultimate goal of living beings.

The Bodhisattva's initial training in accumulating merit or wisdom is the Bodhisattva's path of accumulation; the Bodhisattva's training in accumulating merit or wisdom that is a preparation for attaining the path of seeing is the Bodhisattva's path of preparation; the Bodhisattva's training that is the initial direct realization of emptiness is the Bodhisattva's path of seeing; after completing the path of seeing the Bodhisattva's training that meditates continually on emptiness is the Bodhisattva's path of meditation; and Buddha's omniscient wisdom that is attained through completing all the trainings of Sutra and Tantra is the Path of No More Learning, the state of enlightenment.

TRAINING IN TAKING IN CONJUNCTION WITH THE PRACTICE OF THE SIX PERFECTIONS

There are four main benefits of the meditations on taking and giving: they are powerful methods (1) to purify the potentialities of non-virtuous actions that cause us to experience serious diseases such as cancer; (2) to accumulate a great collection of merit; (3) to ripen our potentiality to be able to benefit all living beings; and (4) to purify our mind.

There was once a Lamrim practitioner called Kharak Gomchen who was seriously afflicted by leprosy. The treatments given by his doctors did not work, and each year his condition grew worse. Finally, his doctors told him that there was nothing they could do to cure his disease. Believing that he would soon die, Gomchen left his home and went to a cemetery to prepare for death. While staying in the cemetery, he concentrated day and night on practising the meditations on taking and giving with strong compassion for all living beings. Through this practice he was completely cured and returned home healthy and with a happy mind. There are many other similar examples.

At the moment we are unable to benefit all living beings but we have the potential for this ability, which is part of our Buddha nature. Through practising the meditations on taking and giving with strong compassion for all living beings, the potential to be able to benefit all living beings will ripen, and when this happens we will become an enlightened being, a Buddha. When we purify our mind through the practices of taking and giving, every spiritual realization will grow easily in our mind. Through contemplating the four main benefits of meditating on taking and giving, we should encourage ourself to practise these meditations sincerely.

'Taking' in this context means taking others' sufferings upon ourself through meditation. When we meditate on taking our motivation should be compassion, thinking:

I must permanently liberate all living beings from their suffering and fears in this life and countless future lives.

In this way, by giving protection we are practising the perfection of giving; by abandoning self-cherishing we are practising the perfection of moral discipline; by willingly accepting any adverse conditions obstructing our practice of taking we are practising the perfection of patience; by applying effort to practising this meditation continually, free from laziness, we are practising the perfection of effort; by concentrating single-pointedly on the meditation on taking, free from distraction, we are practising the perfection of concentration; and by realizing that we ourself, all living beings, and their suffering all exist as mere names and do not inherently exist we are practising the perfection of wisdom. This is how we should train in the meditation on taking in conjunction with practising the six perfections. This is a very profound method of practising the six perfections. We should apply this same method to all other meditations, such as the meditation on death, so that we can quickly make progress along the path to enlightenment.

There are two stages to the meditation on taking:

1 Meditation on taking focusing on all living beings
2 Meditation on taking focusing on particular living beings

MEDITATION ON TAKING FOCUSING ON ALL LIVING BEINGS

In this first stage we focus on the assembly of all living beings without exception, and then think from the depths of our heart:

In their countless future lives these living beings will continually experience without choice the sufferings of humans, animals, hungry ghosts, hell beings, demi-gods and gods. How wonderful it would be if all these living beings were permanently freed from the suffering and fears in this life and countless future lives! May they achieve this. I myself will work for them to achieve this. I must do this.

Thinking in this way, we imagine that the sufferings of all living beings gather together in the aspect of black smoke. This dissolves into our ignorance of self-grasping and self-cherishing at our heart. We then strongly believe that all living beings are permanently freed from suffering, and that our ignorance of self-grasping and self-cherishing is completely destroyed. We meditate on this belief single-pointedly for as long as possible.

With compassion for all living beings we should continually practise this meditation until we experience signs that indicate our mind has been purified. These signs can include the curing of any sickness we may have, the reducing of our delusions, our having a more peaceful and happy mind, the increasing of our faith, correct intention and correct view, and especially the strengthening of our experience of universal compassion.

MEDITATION ON TAKING FOCUSING ON PARTICULAR LIVING BEINGS

In this meditation we can focus, for example, on the assembly of living beings who experience the suffering of sickness. We then think:

These living beings experience the suffering of sickness in this life and in their countless future lives without end. How wonderful it would be if these living beings were permanently freed from sickness! May they achieve this. I myself will work for them to achieve this. I must do this.

Thinking in this way, we imagine that the suffering of sickness of all living beings gathers together in the aspect of black smoke. This dissolves into our ignorance of self-grasping and self-cherishing at our heart. We then strongly believe that all these living beings are permanently freed from sickness, and that our ignorance of self-grasping and self-cherishing is completely destroyed. We meditate on this belief single-pointedly for as long as possible.

In the same way, we can practise the meditation on taking while focusing on a particular individual or group of living beings who are experiencing other sufferings such as poverty, fighting and famine.

We should apply particular effort to developing deep familiarity with the meditation on taking focusing on all living beings. This meditation makes our mind pure, which in turn makes our actions pure so that we become a pure being. If we die with strong compassion for all living beings we will definitely be born in the Pure Land of a Buddha. This is because our compassion that manifests when we are dying will directly cause our potential for taking rebirth in the Pure Land of a Buddha to ripen. This is the good result of a good heart. The result of maintaining the good heart of sincerely wishing to liberate permanently all living beings from suffering is that we ourself will experience permanent liberation from suffering by taking rebirth in the Pure Land of a Buddha.

For example, when Geshe Chekhawa was dying he developed the sincere wish to be reborn in hell in order to help hell beings directly, but he received clear visions that he would be reborn in Sukhavati, the Pure Land of Buddha Amitabha. He told his assistant 'Unfortunately my wish will not be fulfilled.' The assistant asked him, 'What is your wish?', and Geshe Chekhawa replied, 'My wish is to take rebirth in hell so that I can help hell beings directly, but I have seen clear signs that I will be born in the Pure Land of Buddha Amitabha.' Although Geshe Chekhawa wanted to take rebirth in hell, his compassion for all living beings prevented him from taking a lower rebirth; he had no choice but to go to a Buddha's Pure Land where he experienced permanent liberation from suffering. However, although Geshe Chekhawa took rebirth in a Pure Land, he was able to help hell beings through his emanations.

We may think our belief that living beings have attained permanent liberation from suffering through our meditation is incorrect, because living beings have not actually attained this. Although it is true that living beings have not actually attained permanent liberation, our belief is still correct because it arises from our compassion and wisdom. Meditating on this belief will cause our potentiality of being able to liberate all living beings permanently from suffering to ripen quickly, so that we will attain enlightenment quickly. Therefore we should never abandon such a beneficial belief, which is the nature of wisdom. Meditation on taking is the quick path to enlightenment, and has a similar function to Tantric practice. It is said that Tantric realizations can be achieved simply through relying upon correct belief and imagination. This practice is very simple; all we need to do is to become deeply familiar with meditation on correct belief and imagination as presented in Tantra, by applying continual effort.

TRAINING IN GIVING IN CONJUNCTION WITH THE PRACTICE OF THE SIX PERFECTIONS

'Giving' in this context means giving our own happiness to others through meditation. In general, in the cycle of impure life, samsara, there is no real happiness at all. As mentioned previously, the happiness that we normally experience through eating, drinking, sex and so forth is not real happiness, but merely a reduction of a previous problem or dissatisfaction. For example, if the happiness we experience from sex is real happiness, then it would follow that sex itself would be a real cause of happiness. If this were true, then the more we had sex, the more our happiness would increase, but actually the opposite would happen; instead of happiness increasing, our suffering would increase. In *Four Hundred Verses* the Buddhist Master Aryadeva says:

> The experience of suffering will never be changed by
> the same cause,
> But we can see the experience of happiness will be
> changed by the same cause.

This means that, for example, the suffering caused by fire will never be changed into happiness by that fire, but we can see that the happiness caused, for example, by eating will change into suffering just through eating.

How do we meditate on giving? In *Guide to the Bodhisattva's Way of Life* Shantideva says:

> ... to accomplish the welfare of all living beings
> I will transform my body into an enlightened
> wishfulfilling jewel.

We should regard our continuously residing body, our very subtle body, as the real wishfulfilling jewel; this is our Buddha nature through which the wishes of ourself and all other living beings will be fulfilled. We then think:

> *All living beings wish to be happy all the time, but they do not know how to do this. They never experience real happiness, because out of ignorance they destroy their own happiness by developing delusions such as anger and performing non-virtuous actions. How wonderful it would be if all these living beings experienced the pure and everlasting happiness of enlightenment! May they experience this happiness. I will now give my own future happiness of enlightenment to each and every living being.*

Thinking in this way we imagine that from our continuously residing body at our heart we emanate infinite rays of light, which are in nature our future happiness of enlightenment. These reach all living beings of the six realms, and we strongly believe that each and every living being experiences the pure and everlasting happiness of enlightenment. We meditate on this belief single-pointedly for as long as possible. We should continually practise this meditation until we spontaneously believe that all living beings have actually received our future happiness of enlightenment now. Through this practice we are like a Bodhisattva who practises shepherd-like bodhichitta. Just as a shepherd wishes to provide protection and necessary conditions for his flock before he himself relaxes, a Bodhisattva who practises shepherd-like bodhichitta wishes to prepare protection and ultimate happiness for all beings before accomplishing it for himself.

This meditation has four main benefits: (1) it increases our wishing love for all living beings; (2) it ripens our potential ability to benefit all living beings; (3) it accumulates a great collection of merit, or good fortune; and (4) it causes our ordinary appearances and conceptions to cease.

Our future happiness of enlightenment is the result of our generating compassion for all living beings. The meditation on giving brings this future result into the path, and is therefore a quick path to enlightenment that has a similar function to Tantric practice. We should apply great effort to practise this meditation so that we can quickly make progress on the path to enlightenment.

When we are meditating on giving, our motivation should be wishing love. By giving love in this way we are practising the perfection of giving; by abandoning self-cherishing we are practising the perfection of moral discipline; by willingly accepting any adverse conditions obstructing our practice of giving we are practising the perfection of patience; by applying effort to practising this meditation continually, free from laziness, we are practising the perfection of effort; by concentrating single-pointedly on the meditation on giving, free from distraction, we are practising the perfection of concentration; and by realizing that we ourself, all living beings, and their happiness all exist as mere names and do not inherently exist we are practising the perfection of wisdom. This is how we should train in the meditation on giving in conjunction with practising the six perfections.

Training in giving is a special meditation on wishing love that sincerely wishes all living beings to attain real happiness – the pure and everlasting happiness of liberation and enlightenment. As mentioned above, meditation on wishing love is also called 'immeasurable love' because just by meditating on wishing love we receive immeasurable benefits in this life and in countless future lives.

In *Advice from Atisha's Heart* Atisha says:

Friends, until you attain enlightenment, the Spiritual Teacher is indispensable, therefore rely upon the holy Spiritual Guide.

We need to rely upon our Spiritual Guide until we attain enlightenment. The reason for this is very simple. The ultimate goal of human life is to attain enlightenment, and this depends upon continually receiving the special blessings of Buddha through our Spiritual Guide. Buddha attained enlightenment with the sole intention of leading all living beings along the stages of the path to enlightenment through his emanations. Who is his emanation who is leading us along the stages of the path to enlightenment? It is clearly our present Spiritual Teacher who is sincerely and correctly leading us along the paths of renunciation, bodhichitta and the correct view of emptiness by giving these teachings and showing a practical example of someone who is sincerely practising them. With this understanding we should strongly believe that our Spiritual Guide is an emanation of Buddha, and develop and maintain deep faith in him or her.

Atisha also says:

Until you realize ultimate truth, listening is indispensable, therefore listen to the instructions of the Spiritual Guide.

Even if we were mistakenly to see two moons in the sky, this mistaken appearance would remind us that in fact there are not two moons, but only one. In a similar way, if seeing inherently existent things reminds us there are no inherently existent things, this indicates that our understanding of emptiness, ultimate truth, is correct. Until our understanding of emptiness is perfect, and to prevent ourself from falling into one of the two extremes – the extreme of existence and the extreme of non-existence – we should listen to, read and contemplate the instructions of our Spiritual Guide. A more detailed explanation of relying upon our Spiritual Guide can be found in *Joyful Path of Good Fortune*.

All the contemplations and meditations presented in this book should be practised in conjunction with the preliminary practices for meditation presented in Appendix III: *Prayers for Meditation*. These preliminary practices will enable us to purify our mind, accumulate merit and receive the blessings of the enlightened beings, thus ensuring that our meditation practice is successful.

Geshe Kelsang Gyatso Rinpoche

Dedication

Through the virtues accumulated by composing this
  book,
May all suffering quickly cease
And all happiness and joy be fulfilled;
And may holy Dharma flourish for evermore.

Appendix I

The Root Text:

Essence of Wisdom Sutra

The Root Text:

Essence of Wisdom Sutra

In Sanskrit: Bhagavatiprajnaparamitahrdaya
In Tibetan: Chom den de ma she rab kyi pa rol tu jin pai nying po
In English: Essence of the Perfection of Wisdom, the Blessed Mother

Homage to the Perfection of Wisdom, the Blessed Mother.

Thus I have heard. At one time the Blessed One was dwelling in Rajagriha on Massed Vultures Mountain together with a great assembly of monks and nuns, and a great assembly of Bodhisattvas. At that time the Blessed One was absorbed in the concentration of the countless aspects of phenomena, called 'Profound Illumination'.

At that time also the Superior Avalokiteshvara, the Bodhisattva, the Great Being, was looking perfectly at the practice of the profound perfection of wisdom, looking perfectly also at the five aggregates being empty of inherent existence.

Then, through the power of Buddha, the Venerable Shariputra said to the Superior Avalokiteshvara, the Bodhisattva, the Great Being, 'How should a Son of the lineage train who wishes to engage in the practice of the profound perfection of wisdom?'

Thus he spoke, and the Superior Avalokiteshvara, the Bodhisattva, the Great Being, replied to the Venerable Shariputra as follows:

'Shariputra, whatever Son or Daughter of the lineage wishes to engage in the practice of the profound perfection of wisdom should look perfectly like this: subsequently looking perfectly and correctly also at the five aggregates being empty of inherent existence.

'Form is empty; emptiness is form. Emptiness is not other than form; form also is not other than emptiness. Likewise, feeling, discrimination, compositional factors and consciousness are empty.

'Shariputra, like this all phenomena are emptiness, having no characteristics. They are not produced and do not cease. They have no defilement and no separation from defilement. They have no decrease and no increase.

'Therefore, Shariputra, in emptiness there is no form, no feeling, no discrimination, no compositional factors, no consciousness. There is no eye, no ear, no nose, no tongue, no body, no mentality; no form, no sound, no smell, no taste, no tactile object, no phenomenon. There is no eye element and so forth up to no mentality element and also up to no element of mental consciousness. There is no ignorance and no exhaustion of ignorance and so forth up to no ageing and death and no exhaustion of ageing and death. Likewise, there is no suffering, origin, cessation or path; no exalted awareness, no attainment, and also no non-attainment.

'Therefore, Shariputra, because there is no attainment, Bodhisattvas rely upon and abide in the perfection of wisdom; their minds have no obstructions and no fear. Passing utterly beyond perversity, they attain the final nirvana. Also all the Buddhas who reside perfectly in the three times, having relied upon the perfection of wisdom, became manifest and complete Buddhas in the state of unsurpassed, perfect and complete enlightenment.

'Therefore, the mantra of the perfection of wisdom, the mantra of great knowledge, the unsurpassed mantra, the equal-to-the-unequalled mantra, the mantra that thoroughly pacifies all suffering, since it is not false, should be known as the truth. The mantra of the perfection of wisdom is proclaimed:

TAYATHA OM GATE GATE PARAGATE PARASAMGATE BODHI SÖHA

'Shariputra, a Bodhisattva, a Great Being, should train in the profound perfection of wisdom like this.'

Then the Blessed One arose from that concentration and said to the Superior Avalokiteshvara, the Bodhisattva, the Great Being, that he had spoken well: 'Good, good, O Son of the lineage. It is like that. Since it is like that, just as you have revealed, in that way the profound perfection of wisdom should be practised, and the Tathagatas will also rejoice.'

When the Blessed One had said this, the Venerable Shariputra, the Superior Avalokiteshvara, the Bodhisattva, the Great Being, and that entire circle of disciples as well as the worldly beings – gods, humans, demi-gods and spirits – were delighted and highly praised what had been spoken by the Blessed One.

Appendix II

The Condensed Meaning
of the Commentary

The Condensed Meaning
of the Commentary

The commentary to the *Heart Sutra* has two parts:

1 The explanation of the direct meaning of the Sutra
2 The explanation of the hidden meaning of the Sutra

Part One: The explanation of the direct meaning of the Sutra has three parts:

1 The meaning of the title
2 The homage of the translators
3 The explanation of the main body of the Sutra

The explanation of the main body of the Sutra has three parts:

1 The common explanation of the background to the Sutra
2 The uncommon explanation of the background to the Sutra
3 The explanation of the actual Sutra

The common explanation of the background to the Sutra has four parts:

1 The speaker of the Sutra
2 The time when the Sutra was delivered

3 The place where the Sutra was delivered
4 To whom the Sutra was spoken

The explanation of the actual Sutra has four parts:

1 The question of Shariputra
2 The answers by Avalokiteshvara
3 The approval of the answers by Buddha
4 The followers are pleased and take the teachings to
   heart

The answers by Avalokiteshvara has six parts:

1 A brief explanation of how to train in the
   perfection of wisdom on the paths of accumulation
   and preparation
2 An extensive explanation of how to train in the
   perfection of wisdom on the paths of accumulation
   and preparation
3 An explanation of how to train in the perfection of
   wisdom on the path of seeing
4 An explanation of how to train in the perfection of
   wisdom on the path of meditation
5 An explanation of how to attain the Path of No
   More Learning
6 Conclusion

An extensive explanation of how to train in the perfection of
wisdom on the paths of accumulation and preparation has
two parts:

1 The explanation of the four profundities of the
   aggregate of form
2 The explanation of the four profundities of the
   aggregates of feeling and so forth

The explanation of the four profundities of the aggregate of form has four parts:

1 The explanation of the profundity of the ultimate of the aggregate of form
2 The explanation of the profundity of the conventional of the aggregate of form
3 The explanation of the profundity of the union of the two truths of the aggregate of form
4 The explanation of the profundity of the nominal distinction of the two truths of the aggregate of form

An explanation of how to train in the perfection of wisdom on the path of meditation has five parts:

1 Recognizing samsara
2 Who experiences suffering
3 How we experience suffering
4 How we wander in samsara
5 The attainment of liberation or nirvana

Part Two: The explanation of the hidden meaning of the Sutra has four parts:

1 Preliminary explanation
2 Protector Nagarjuna
3 Arya Asanga
4 The stages of the vast path: the hidden meaning of the *Heart Sutra*

The stages of the vast path: the hidden meaning of the *Heart Sutra* has three parts:

1 The path of a person of initial scope
2 The path of a person of middling scope
3 The path of a person of great scope

The path of a person of initial scope has five parts:

1 The preciousness of our human life
2 What does our death mean?
3 The dangers of lower rebirth
4 Going for refuge
5 What is karma?

The path of a person of middling scope has four parts:

1 What we should know
2 What we should abandon
3 What we should practise
4 What we should attain

The path of a person of great scope has two parts:

1 The supreme good heart – bodhichitta
2 Training in the path of bodhichitta

The supreme good heart – bodhichitta has five parts:

1 Training in affectionate love
2 Training in cherishing love
3 Training in wishing love
4 Training in universal compassion
5 Training in actual bodhichitta

Training in cherishing love has two parts:

1 Equalizing self and others
2 Exchanging self with others

Exchanging self with others has three parts:

1 Contemplating the disadvantages of self-cherishing
2 Contemplating the advantages of cherishing others
3 The actual training in exchanging self with others

Training in the path of bodhichitta has three parts:

1 Training in the six perfections
2 Training in taking in conjunction with the practice of the six perfections
3 Training in giving in conjunction with the practice of the six perfections

Training in taking in conjunction with the practice of the six perfections has two parts:

1 Meditation on taking focusing on all living beings
2 Meditation on taking focusing on particular living beings

Appendix III

Liberating Prayer

and

Prayers for Meditation

Liberating Prayer

PRAISE TO BUDDHA SHAKYAMUNI

O Blessed One, Shakyamuni Buddha,
Precious treasury of compassion,
Bestower of supreme inner peace,

You, who love all beings without exception,
Are the source of happiness and goodness;
And you guide us to the liberating path.

Your body is a wishfulfilling jewel,
Your speech is supreme, purifying nectar,
And your mind is refuge for all living beings.

With folded hands I turn to you,
Supreme unchanging friend,
I request from the depths of my heart:

Please give me the light of your wisdom
To dispel the darkness of my mind
And to heal my mental continuum.

Please nourish me with your goodness,
That I in turn may nourish all beings
With an unceasing banquet of delight.

Through your compassionate intention,
Your blessings and virtuous deeds,
And my strong wish to rely upon you,

May all suffering quickly cease
And all happiness and joy be fulfilled;
And may holy Dharma flourish for evermore.

Colophon: This prayer was composed by Venerable Geshe
Kelsang Gyatso and is recited at the beginning of teachings,
meditations and prayers in Kadampa Buddhist Centres
throughout the world.

Prayers for Meditation

BRIEF PREPARATORY PRAYERS FOR MEDITATION

Introduction

We all have the potential to gain realizations of all the stages of the path to enlightenment. These potentials are like seeds in the field of our mind, and our meditation practice is like cultivating these seeds. However, our meditation practice will be successful only if we make good preparations beforehand.

If we want to cultivate external crops, we begin by making careful preparations. First, we remove from the soil anything that might obstruct their growth, such as stones and weeds. Second, we enrich the soil with compost or fertilizer to give it the strength to sustain growth. Third, we provide warm, moist conditions to enable the seeds to germinate and the plants to grow. In the same way, to cultivate our inner crops of Dharma realizations we must also begin by making careful preparations.

First, we must purify our mind to eliminate the negative karma we have accumulated in the past, because if we do not purify this karma it will obstruct the growth of Dharma realizations. Second, we need to give our mind the strength to support the growth of Dharma realizations by accumulating merit. Third, we need to activate and sustain the growth of Dharma realizations by receiving the blessings of the holy beings.

The brief prayers that follow contain the essence of these three preparations. For more information on them, see *The New Meditation Handbook* or *Joyful Path of Good Fortune*.

Geshe Kelsang Gyatso
1987

Prayers for Meditation

Going for refuge

I and all sentient beings, until we achieve enlightenment,
Go for refuge to Buddha, Dharma and Sangha.

(3x, 7x, 100x, or more)

Generating bodhichitta

Through the virtues I collect by giving and other
perfections,
May I become a Buddha for the benefit of all.
(3x)

Generating the four immeasurables

May everyone be happy,
May everyone be free from misery,
May no one ever be separated from their happiness,
May everyone have equanimity, free from hatred and
attachment.

Visualizing the Field for Accumulating Merit

In the space before me is the living Buddha Shakyamuni
surrounded by all the Buddhas and Bodhisattvas, like the
full moon surrounded by stars.

Prayer of seven limbs

With my body, speech and mind, humbly I prostrate,
And make offerings both set out and imagined.
I confess my wrong deeds from all time,
And rejoice in the virtues of all.
Please stay until samsara ceases,
And turn the Wheel of Dharma for us.
I dedicate all virtues to great enlightenment.

Offering the mandala

The ground sprinkled with perfume and spread
    with flowers,
The Great Mountain, four lands, sun and moon,
Seen as a Buddha Land and offered thus,
May all beings enjoy such Pure Lands.

I offer without any sense of loss
The objects that give rise to my attachment, hatred
    and confusion,
My friends, enemies and strangers, our bodies and
    enjoyments;
Please accept these and bless me to be released
    directly from the three poisons.

IDAM GURU RATNA MANDALAKAM NIRYATAYAMI

Prayer of the Stages of the Path

The path begins with strong reliance
On my kind Teacher, source of all good;
O Bless me with this understanding
To follow him with great devotion.

This human life with all its freedoms,
Extremely rare, with so much meaning;
O Bless me with this understanding
All day and night to seize its essence.

My body, like a water bubble,
Decays and dies so very quickly;
After death come results of karma,
Just like the shadow of a body.

With this firm knowledge and remembrance
Bless me to be extremely cautious,
Always avoiding harmful actions
And gathering abundant virtue.

Samsara's pleasures are deceptive,
Give no contentment, only torment;
So please bless me to strive sincerely
To gain the bliss of perfect freedom.

O Bless me so that from this pure thought
Come mindfulness and greatest caution,
To keep as my essential practice
The doctrine's root, the Pratimoksha.

Just like myself all my kind mothers
Are drowning in samsara's ocean;
O So that I may soon release them,
Bless me to train in bodhichitta.

But I cannot become a Buddha
By this alone without three ethics;

So bless me with the strength to practise
The Bodhisattva's ordination.

By pacifying my distractions
And analyzing perfect meanings,
Bless me to quickly gain the union
Of special insight and quiescence.

When I become a pure container
Through common paths, bless me to enter
The essence practice of good fortune,
The supreme vehicle, Vajrayana.

The two attainments both depend on
My sacred vows and my commitments;
Bless me to understand this clearly
And keep them at the cost of my life.

By constant practice in four sessions,
The way explained by holy Teachers,
O Bless me to gain both the stages,
Which are the essence of the Tantras.

May those who guide me on the good path,
And my companions all have long lives;
Bless me to pacify completely
All obstacles, outer and inner.

May I always find perfect Teachers,
And take delight in holy Dharma,
Accomplish all grounds and paths swiftly,
And gain the state of Vajradhara.

Receiving blessings and purifying

From the hearts of all the holy beings, streams of light and nectar flow down, granting blessings and purifying.

At this point, we begin the actual contemplation and meditation. After the meditation, we dedicate our merit while reciting the following prayers:

Dedication prayers

Through the virtues I have collected
By practising the stages of the path,
May all living beings find the opportunity
To practise in the same way.

May everyone experience
The happiness of humans and gods,
And quickly attain enlightenment,
So that samsara is finally extinguished.

Prayers for the Virtuous Tradition

So that the tradition of Je Tsongkhapa,
The King of the Dharma, may flourish,
May all obstacles be pacified
And may all favourable conditions abound.

Through the two collections of myself and others
Gathered throughout the three times,
May the doctrine of Conqueror Losang Dragpa
Flourish for evermore.

The nine-line *Migtsema* prayer

Tsongkhapa, crown ornament of the scholars of the Land
of the Snows,
You are Buddha Shakyamuni and Vajradhara, the source
of all attainments,
Avalokiteshvara, the treasury of unobservable compassion,
Manjushri, the supreme stainless wisdom,
And Vajrapani, the destroyer of the hosts of maras.
O Venerable Guru-Buddha, synthesis of all Three Jewels,
With my body, speech and mind, respectfully I make
requests:
Please grant your blessings to ripen and liberate myself
and others,
And bestow the common and supreme attainments.　　(3x)

Colophon: This sadhana or ritual prayer for
spiritual attainments was compiled by
Venerable Geshe Kelsang Gyatso
based on traditional sources.

Appendix IV

Explanation of the Twelve Sources, Eighteen Elements and Twelve Dependent-related Links

Explanation of the Twelve Sources, Eighteen Elements and Twelve Dependent-related Links

All phenomena are included in the twelve sources, which are:

(1) Eye source
(2) Ear source
(3) Nose source
(4) Tongue source
(5) Body source
(6) Mentality source
(7) Form source
(8) Sound source
(9) Smell source
(10) Taste source
(11) Tactile object source
(12) Phenomena source

'Eye source' refers to the source of eye consciousness. 'Eye', 'eye sense power' and 'eye source' are synonymous. Normally, we point to our eyeball and say, 'This is my eye'; but if the eyeball itself were the eye it would follow that a blind person who had eyeballs would possess eyes and could therefore see. Our eye – our eye source or eye sense power – is not physical form but an inner potential power located in the very centre of the eyeball, whose main function is to generate an eye consciousness directly. It is a very hidden object. The eye source, ear source, nose source, tongue source and the body source possess form but they are not physical form, in the same way that a person called John, for example, possesses form but is not physical form. They are inner potential powers located in the very centre of the organs of the eyes, ears, nose and tongue, and throughout the body respectively, and their main functions are to generate directly eye, ear, nose, tongue and body consciousnesses respectively.

We cannot understand these five sources or sense powers through using logical reasons or with direct perceivers because they are very hidden objects. We can understand them only by studying Buddha's teachings. The five sources or five sense powers are extremely important for our daily experience. For example, without an eye sense power we cannot generate an eye consciousness with which to see forms, without an ear sense power we cannot generate an ear consciousness with which to hear sounds, without a nose sense power and a tongue sense power we cannot generate nose and tongue consciousnesses with which to smell odours and experience tastes, and without a body sense power we cannot generate a body consciousness with which to experience tactile objects. 'Mentality source' is synonymous with 'mental power' and is a mental potential power whose main function is to generate directly mental consciousness with which we can understand various kinds of phenomena. It too is a very hidden object.

The last six sources are: form source – the object of the eye source; sound source – the object of the ear source; smell source – the object of the nose source; taste source – the object of the tongue source; tactile object source – the object of the body source; and phenomena source – the object of the mentality source. They are called 'sources' because they are the source of the process for generating consciousnesses.

EIGHTEEN ELEMENTS

From another point of view, all phenomena are included in the eighteen elements, which are:

(1) Eye element
(2) Ear element
(3) Nose element
(4) Tongue element
(5) Body element
(6) Mentality element
(7) Form element
(8) Sound element
(9) Smell element
(10) Taste element
(11) Tactile object element
(12) Phenomena element
(13) Element of eye consciousness
(14) Element of ear consciousness

(15) Element of nose consciousness

(16) Element of tongue consciousness

(17) Element of body consciousness

(18) Element of mental consciousness

As mentioned previously in Part One, Buddha explained the eighteen elements to show how living beings experience suffering. They are called 'elements' because they are inseparable from their own nature, as indicated by the Tibetan word for element (kham). 'Eye element' is synonymous with 'eye source' and 'eye sense power'; and likewise the ear, nose, tongue and body elements are synonymous with their respective sources and sense powers. 'Mentality element' and 'mental power' are synonyms.

Forms, sounds, smells, tastes, tactile objects and phenomena are objects of the first six elements and the last six elements respectively.

Living beings experience suffering in the following way. Because of our eye sense power, ear sense power and so forth meeting with their objects – forms, sounds and so forth – we develop an eye consciousness, ear consciousness and so forth that perceive inherently existent things. For us this automatically gives rise to a mind that believes these things to be inherently existent. This is our mind of self-grasping ignorance. Because of this ignorance we experience various kinds of sufferings and problems, which are mistaken appearances or hallucinations, just as we experience things in dreams.

TWELVE DEPENDENT-RELATED LINKS

The twelve dependent-related links are:

(1) Dependent-related ignorance
(2) Dependent-related compositional actions
(3) Dependent-related consciousness
(4) Dependent-related name and form
(5) Dependent-related six sources
(6) Dependent-related contact
(7) Dependent-related feeling
(8) Dependent-related craving
(9) Dependent-related grasping
(10) Dependent-related existence
(11) Dependent-related birth
(12) Dependent-related ageing and death

The dependent-related ignorance that is the first link is a mind of self-grasping that motivates a person to create an action that is a cause of taking rebirth in samsara. Such a mind is called 'ignorance' because it grasps phenomena as inherently existent through being ignorant of their true nature.

The second link, dependent-related compositional actions, is an action, or karma, that is a projecting cause of taking a rebirth in samsara. Since its effect is to project, or throw, us into a rebirth in samsara it is also called 'throwing karma'. Although a compositional action is motivated by the first link, dependent-related ignorance, it may be virtuous or non-virtuous depending on the intention accompanying it. A virtuous compositional action leads to a cyclic rebirth in one of the three higher realms, whereas a non-virtuous compositional action leads to a cyclic rebirth in one of the three lower realms.

The third link, dependent-related consciousness, does not refer to consciousness in general but only to the root mental consciousness that receives the imprint of a dependent-related compositional action. Each compositional action, such as the non-virtuous action of killing, leaves an imprint on our root consciousness. This imprint remains in our continuum of consciousness as a seed-like potency until the circumstances arise that activate it to produce the effect of a rebirth in samsara.

The fourth link is dependent-related name and form. This link is the five aggregates of a person at the moment of rebirth – form being the form aggregate and name being the other four aggregates. We can take our own birth as an example. We took our present rebirth as a human being when our consciousness entered the fertilized ovum in our mother's womb. At that moment, we comprised five rudimentary aggregates. Our form aggregate was the physical form of the fertilized ovum, and the remaining aggregates of feeling and so forth were also present. Our five aggregates at that moment are an example of the fourth link, dependent-related name and form. The last four aggregates are called 'name' because they serve as a basis for naming or identifying a person even in the case of a person in the formless realm, who lacks a form aggregate.

Dependent-related six sources, which are the fifth link, are the five sense powers and the mental power when they first develop after rebirth. In the case of our present rebirth as a human being we had the mental power and body sense power from the moment of conception, but the remaining four sense powers of eye, ear, nose and tongue were generated gradually as we developed in the womb.

The sixth link is dependent-related contact. Contact is a mental factor that accompanies every moment of consciousness. It arises from the coming together of an object, a sense power and a consciousness. Its function is to perceive an object as pleasant, unpleasant or neutral.

In dependence upon contact we develop the seventh link, dependent-related feeling. Whereas contact perceives an object as pleasant, unpleasant or neutral, feeling is the mental factor that experiences the object as pleasant, unpleasant or neutral. Whenever we cognize an object we generate a pleasant, unpleasant or neutral feeling.

Dependent-related craving, the eighth link, is a particular form of attachment that nourishes, or activates, the potentiality to take our next rebirth that was left on our consciousness by a previous dependent-related compositional action. This type of attachment occurs at the time of our death. Normally at that time we develop a strong attachment towards what we grasp as 'me', and towards our body, friends, possessions and so forth. This craving activates the potential to take our next rebirth.

The ninth link is dependent-related grasping. This is also a type of attachment but it is more intense than craving. Craving can be compared with the strong desire to smoke a cigarette that is developed by someone who has recently given up smoking. Grasping is like that desire when it becomes so strong that it forces the person out of his house in search of a cigarette. Dependent-related grasping is the grasping that develops after dependent-related craving, and it activates more powerfully the potential to take our next rebirth.

The tenth link, dependent-related existence, is the mental factor intention that is induced by the previous links of craving and grasping. It is called 'existence' because it is the immediate cause of taking a new rebirth in cyclic existence, samsara. This is an example of the name of an effect being given to its cause. Intention in general is mental action, and the nature of intention determines whether a mind is virtuous or not. If the mental factor intention is virtuous the mind that it accompanies is necessarily virtuous. Conversely, if the intention is non-virtuous the mind it accompanies is also non-virtuous.

Although craving and grasping are delusions they can induce a virtuous mind at the time of death. For example, they can induce a mind that goes for refuge to and prays to holy beings. In such a case the tenth link, dependent-related existence, is a virtuous action and it is certain that an imprint left by a virtuous compositional action will be activated. The person will then take a fortunate rebirth as a human or a god. On the other hand, if the craving and grasping induce a non-virtuous mind, such as anger, then the tenth link is a non-virtuous action and a potential to take a rebirth in the lower realms will be activated.

The eleventh link is dependent-related birth. It refers to the moment when a consciousness takes a new existence. In the case of rebirth as a human being, dependent-related birth refers to the entry of a consciousness into a fertilized ovum in the mother's womb.

From the second moment of a new rebirth the process of ageing begins, and it continues until death. The final link, dependent-related ageing and death, is this process of ageing and death itself.

These twelve dependent-related links reveal the process whereby we remain chained to a cycle of uncontrolled rebirth and death with its associated sufferings. The fundamental cause of this uncontrolled process is the first link, ignorance, which is a mind that grasps at inherent existence. Under the control of ignorance, we perform the virtuous or non-virtuous actions that are the causes for us to take rebirth in higher or lower realms of samsara. These actions are compositional actions, the second link. A compositional action leaves an imprint on our mind, and the consciousness that receives this imprint is the third link. These first three links are sometimes called 'projecting causes' because they act as the causes that project us into a future uncontrolled rebirth. The three projecting causes are also called the 'distant causes' of rebirth because, although they are the causes of a future rebirth, there may be many intervening lifetimes before that particular rebirth is actualized.

The next four links are called 'projected effects' and explain our development after having been projected into a new rebirth. The fourth link indicates that the basis of imputing our new identity is our new aggregates, name and form. In dependence upon our aggregates, the fifth link, the six sources, are formed. The six sources are the six powers and as a result of these the sixth link, contact, arises. In dependence upon contact we develop pleasant, unpleasant or neutral feelings, the seventh link.

The next three links indicate how the potential power to take our next rebirth is actualized, and so they are called 'actualizing causes'. These three links are also called 'close causes' of rebirth because they are the causes that immediately precede a rebirth. In dependence upon previous feelings, the eighth and ninth links, craving and grasping, arise as death approaches. These activate the potential to take our next rebirth, leading to the development of the tenth link, existence, which is the mental action that carries us towards our next rebirth.

The last two links are called 'actualized effects' because they are the effects of the actualizing causes. The three actualizing causes activate a particular potential to take rebirth, giving rise to the eleventh link, birth. As a result of birth within samsara the last link, ageing and death, occurs. The last two links also imply all the other sufferings of samsara, such as sickness, that occur between birth and death.

If we contemplate the twelve links in this sequence, from ignorance to ageing and death, we can understand the step-by-step development of cyclic rebirth and the sufferings associated with it. If we contemplate the twelve dependent-related links in reverse order we can trace back the causes of our suffering. The last link combines two of the gross sufferings that we experience, ageing and death, but all our other sufferings are also implied. The cause of these sufferings is uncontrolled rebirth, the eleventh link. Birth results from the tenth link, existence, which is caused by grasping and craving, the ninth and eighth links. These two forms of attachment result from previous feelings, the seventh link. Feelings arise in dependence upon contact, the sixth link, which in turn depends upon the six sources, the fifth link. The six sources develop in dependence upon the five aggregates at the time of birth, which are the fourth link, name and form. The cause of taking these aggregates is an imprint carried by consciousness. The consciousness that received this imprint is the third link. The imprint on the consciousness is left by a compositional action, the second link. The root motivating force of compositional actions is ignorance, the mind that grasps at inherent existence. In this way, we can trace back the cause of all suffering to ignorance, the first of the twelve links.

Thus, by contemplating the twelve links in reverse order we can realize that we experience suffering again and again because we have taken cyclic rebirth, and that the fundamental cause of this miserable process is ignorance. Realizing that the cause of all suffering is cyclic rebirth will lead us to develop the mind that wishes definitely to leave samsara. This mind is called 'renunciation'. Realizing that ignorance is the root cause of cyclic rebirth we will understand that the method to attain liberation from samsara is to dispel our ignorance. The direct antidote to ignorance is the wisdom that realizes emptiness. With persistent effort using correct methods we can develop this wisdom. If we then continue to meditate on emptiness with the motivation of renunciation and bodhichitta, our dependent-related ignorance, the first of the twelve links, will gradually diminish and eventually cease.

The complete cessation of dependent-related ignorance is the dependent-related exhaustion of ignorance. If we attain this exhaustion of ignorance our actions will no longer be controlled by delusions and therefore we will attain the dependent-related exhaustion of compositional actions. This leads to the dependent-related exhaustion of consciousness and so forth up to the dependent-related exhaustion of ageing and death. Thus, by attaining the exhaustion of ignorance, we overcome cyclic rebirth and cut the continuum of suffering. The cessation of the continuum of suffering is liberation, the state beyond sorrow, or nirvana. There is therefore a second set of twelve dependent-related links, from the exhaustion of ignorance up to the exhaustion of ageing and death. The first set of twelve links from ignorance up to ageing and death are called the 'twelve dependent-related links of the side of delusion' and the twelve links from the exhaustion of ignorance up to the exhaustion of ageing and death are called the 'twelve dependent-related links of the perfectly purified side'. The former explain the development of cyclic rebirth and suffering, and the latter explain their cessation and the attainment of liberation.

The twelve links of the perfectly purified side are the mere cessation of the twelve links of the side of delusion. For example, dependent-related exhaustion of consciousness is not the cessation of consciousness in general but the complete cessation of consciousness that receives imprints of compositional actions. Similarly, dependent-related exhaustion of feeling is merely the cessation of feelings that are contaminated by delusions. If we attain liberation, we still have feelings but these feelings are not contaminated and do not lead to craving and grasping at the time of death.

Having attained liberation, we will no longer be projected into a rebirth under the control of delusions, but we will experience uncontaminated rebirth. An uncontaminated rebirth does not have the nature of suffering and does not give rise to suffering in the future. Most Hinayana Foe Destroyers take an uncontaminated rebirth in a Pure Land and remain in a quiescent state of peace for a very long time. On the other hand, high Bodhisattvas continue to take rebirth among beings within samsara in order to benefit them. Such a rebirth is not contaminated because it arises through the force of compassion and not through the force of delusions. If a high Bodhisattva takes rebirth as a human being he or she will appear to others as an ordinary human being, but such a Bodhisattva is completely free from the sufferings of samsara and works joyfully for the sake of others.

By contemplating the twelve dependent-related links of the perfectly purified side our mind will be uplifted because we will understand that we can completely abandon suffering and its causes by overcoming our ignorance that grasps at the inherent existence of phenomena.

This explanation of the twelve sources, eighteen elements and twelve dependent-related links is presented in a way that is simple and easy to understand, and is based on Buddha's teachings.

Geshe Kelsang Gyatso
September 2011

Appendix V

The Great Mother:

A METHOD TO OVERCOME HINDRANCES
AND OBSTACLES BY RECITING THE
ESSENCE OF WISDOM SUTRA
(THE *HEART SUTRA*)

The Great Mother:

A METHOD TO OVERCOME HINDRANCES
AND OBSTACLES BY RECITING THE
ESSENCE OF WISDOM SUTRA
(THE *HEART SUTRA*)

INTRODUCTION

All living beings wish to be happy but again and again they
find their attainment of happiness frustrated by obstacles or
hindrances, both external and internal. External hindrances
can arise from animate objects such as malevolent humans
and wild animals; or from inanimate objects such as the four
external elements of earth, water, fire and wind, which can
give rise to earthquakes, floods, destructive fires and hurri-
canes. Internal hindrances arise from causes within our body
and mind. If our four internal elements are in a state of har-
monious equilibrium our body is healthy, but when they are
out of balance our body experiences a variety of problems
and diseases. If our mind is filled with negative thoughts and
delusions, such as desirous attachment, anger and ignorance,
we experience great harm and suffering as a result. They prevent us from maintaining a peaceful mind, and also destroy
whatever happiness we may have gained.

The main obstacles that hinder our progress to liberation
and enlightenment can be summarized as the four maras,

'mara' being a Sanskrit word meaning 'demon'. The four maras are: the mara of the delusions, the mara of the aggregates, the mara of the Lord of Death, and Devaputra mara. Anyone who conquers these four maras completely is a Buddha, or 'Conqueror'.

All the suffering we experience arises as a result of our delusions and the actions we create under their influence. As well as disrupting our temporary happiness and peace, delusions also hinder our progress towards the ultimate happiness of liberation and enlightenment.

Our contaminated aggregates are the very nature of samsara and the basis of all our suffering. For as long as we have these aggregates we will be unable to attain liberation.

The mara of the Lord of Death refers to ordinary, uncontrolled death, which deprives us of the chance to complete our spiritual practice. Unless we have thoroughly purified our negative actions and gained firm control over our body, speech and mind, we cannot be confident that after death we will not fall into a lower rebirth where spiritual practice is impossible and escape very difficult.

The Devaputra maras are actual beings such as Black Ishvara who interfere with our spiritual progress to liberation and enlightenment. For example, when Buddha Shakyamuni was about to demonstrate the attainment of enlightenment under the Bodhi Tree it was the Devaputra maras who tried to disturb him. Buddha overcame these interferences through the force of his meditative concentration on love.

If we are to attain temporary happiness while we remain in samsara, and if we are to progress unimpeded towards the ultimate happiness of liberation and enlightenment, we need a special method for averting and overcoming hindrances in general and the four maras in particular. The following practice involves the recitation and contemplation of the *Essence of Wisdom Sutra*, or *Heart Sutra*, and can be used to overcome both external and internal hindrances, either for one's own sake or for the sake of others. An explanation of how to do this practice can be found in Appendix VI.

The extent to which we are successful in overcoming obstacles through this practice depends on the strength of our faith. We can increase our faith by contemplating illustrations of the practice such as the time when the god Indra overcame the anger and jealousy of the demi-gods who were attacking him, or the time when Lama Ukarwa averted the murderous threat of a black magician. Accounts of these can be found in the short commentary to the practice of *The Great Mother* in Appendix VI.

The Great Mother

Going for refuge

I and all sentient beings, until we achieve enlightenment,
Go for refuge to Buddha, Dharma and Sangha.   (3x)

Generating bodhichitta

Through the virtues I collect by giving and other
    perfections,
May I become a Buddha for the benefit of all.   (3x)

Preliminaries

NAMO Guru, Teacher, Blessed One, and the Great Mother
    Prajnaparamita,
Surrounded by your Sons, the Buddhas of the ten
    directions and all Bodhisattvas;
I prostrate to this assembly, make offerings and go for
    refuge,
Please empower me with your blessings.   (3x)

Reciting the *Essence of Wisdom Sutra*

Homage to the perfection of wisdom, the Blessed Mother.

Thus I have heard. At one time the Blessed One was dwelling in Rajagriha on Massed Vultures Mountain together with a great assembly of monks and nuns, and a great assembly of Bodhisattvas. At that time the Blessed One was absorbed in the concentration of the countless aspects of phenomena, called 'Profound Illumination'.

At that time also the Superior Avalokiteshvara, the Bodhisattva, the Great Being, was looking perfectly at the practice of the profound perfection of wisdom, looking perfectly also at the five aggregates being empty of inherent existence.

Then, through the power of Buddha, the Venerable Shariputra said to the Superior Avalokiteshvara, the Bodhisattva, the Great Being, 'How should a Son of the lineage train who wishes to engage in the practice of the profound perfection of wisdom?'

Thus he spoke, and the Superior Avalokiteshvara, the Bodhisattva, the Great Being, replied to the Venerable Shariputra as follows:

'Shariputra, whatever Son or Daughter of the lineage wishes to engage in the practice of the profound perfection of wisdom should look perfectly like this: subsequently looking perfectly and correctly also at the five aggregates being empty of inherent existence.

'Form is empty; emptiness is form. Emptiness is not other than form; form also is not other than emptiness. Likewise, feeling, discrimination, compositional factors and consciousness are empty.

'Shariputra, like this all phenomena are emptiness, having no characteristics. They are not produced and do not cease. They have no defilement and no separation from defilement. They have no decrease and no increase.

'Therefore, Shariputra, in emptiness there is no form, no feeling, no discrimination, no compositional factors, no consciousness. There is no eye, no ear, no nose, no tongue, no body, no mentality; no form, no sound, no smell, no taste, no tactile object, no phenomenon. There is no eye element and so forth up to no mentality element and also up to no element of mental consciousness. There is no ignorance and no exhaustion of ignorance and so forth up to no ageing and death and no exhaustion of ageing and death. Likewise, there is no suffering, origin, cessation or path; no exalted awareness, no attainment, and also no non-attainment.

'Therefore, Shariputra, because there is no attainment, Bodhisattvas rely upon and abide in the perfection of wisdom; their minds have no obstructions and no fear. Passing utterly beyond perversity, they attain the final nirvana. Also all the Buddhas who reside perfectly in the three times, having relied upon the perfection of wisdom, became manifest and complete Buddhas in the state of unsurpassed, perfect and complete enlightenment.

'Therefore, the mantra of the perfection of wisdom, the mantra of great knowledge, the unsurpassed mantra, the equal-to-the-unequalled mantra, the mantra that thoroughly pacifies all suffering, since it is not false, should be known as the truth. The mantra of the perfection of wisdom is proclaimed:

TAYATHA OM GATE GATE PARAGATE PARASAMGATE BODHI SÖHA

'Shariputra, a Bodhisattva, a Great Being, should train in the profound perfection of wisdom like this.'

Then the Blessed One arose from that concentration and said to the Superior Avalokiteshvara, the Bodhisattva, the Great Being, that he had spoken well: 'Good, good, O Son of the lineage. It is like that. Since it is like that, just as you have revealed, in that way the profound perfection of wisdom should be practised, and the Tathagatas will also rejoice.'

When the Blessed One had said this, the Venerable Shariputra, the Superior Avalokiteshvara, the Bodhisattva, the Great Being, and that entire circle of disciples as well as the worldly beings – gods, humans, demi-gods, and spirits – were delighted and highly praised what had been spoken by the Blessed One.

Reciting the mantra

TAYATHA OM GATE GATE PARAGATE PARASAMGATE BODHI
   SÖHA   (3x, 7x, etc.)

Requests to overcome hindrances

Great Mother Prajnaparamita, and all the Buddhas and Bodhisattvas of the ten directions, through the power of your blessings may these true words of mine be achieved. Just as before, when by contemplating the profound meaning of the perfection of wisdom and reciting its words, Indra overcame all the harm of maras, non-humans and so forth, in the same way, by my contemplating the profound meaning of the perfection of wisdom and reciting its words,

May all the harm of maras, non-humans,	
and so forth be overcome.	(clap)
May they become non-existent.	(clap)
May they be pacified.	(clap)
May they be thoroughly pacified.	(clap)

Dedication and prayer

May all kinds of interferences, diseases and possessing
   spirits be pacified.
May I be separated from unfavourable conditions
And may I achieve favourable conditions and everything
   excellent.
Through this fortune may the happiness of enlightenment
   be fulfilled.

Prayers for the Virtuous Tradition

So that the tradition of Je Tsongkhapa,
The King of the Dharma, may flourish,
May all obstacles be pacified
And may all favourable conditions abound.

Through the two collections of myself and others
Gathered throughout the three times,
May the doctrine of Conqueror Losang Dragpa
Flourish for evermore.

The nine-line *Migtsema* prayer

Tsongkhapa, crown ornament of the scholars of the Land
   of the Snows,
You are Buddha Shakyamuni and Vajradhara, the source
   of all attainments,
Avalokiteshvara, the treasury of unobservable compassion,
Manjushri, the supreme stainless wisdom,
And Vajrapani, the destroyer of the hosts of maras.
O Venerable Guru-Buddha, synthesis of all Three Jewels,
With my body, speech and mind, respectfully I make
   requests:

Please grant your blessings to ripen and liberate myself
and others,
And bestow the common and supreme attainments.   (3x)

Colophon: This sadhana or ritual prayer for spiritual
attainments of Great Mother Prajnaparamita was
compiled by Venerable Geshe Kelsang Gyatso
based on traditional sources.

Appendix VI

A Short Commentary to the
Practice of *The Great Mother*

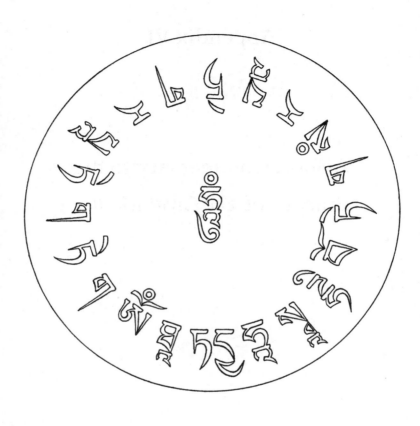

The mantra of the perfection of wisdom:
TAYATHA OM GATE GATE PARAGATE PARASAMGATE BODHI SÖHA

A Short Commentary to the Practice of *The Great Mother*

The practice of *The Great Mother* is a powerful method to avert and overcome all our hindrances and obstacles, both to worldly happiness and to the attainment of liberation.

In our life we experience innumerable hindrances and obstacles to the fulfilment of our wishes. Because of our strong attachment to the fulfilment of our own wishes, whenever our wishes – especially those we consider important – are not fulfilled we experience mental pain, discouragement and many other problems. Just as our desires are immeasurable, so too are our hindrances and obstacles. We experience disappointment after disappointment in this life, and in life after life. Sometimes we may fulfil our desires for worldly attainments, such as reputation, a high position, relationships, wealth and so forth, but these attainments are deceptive; they continually give rise to many undesirable problems. And if we die tomorrow, our reputation, position, relationships and wealth will provide nothing for our future benefit. Worldly attainments are hollow. The only non-deceptive attainment is the supreme permanent peace of mind through which we experience pure happiness throughout our life and in life after life. This attainment is called 'nirvana'.

Although there are innumerable hindrances and obstacles to attaining nirvana or liberation we can overcome them all through receiving Buddha's blessings and increasing our wisdom. The supreme method to receive Buddha's blessings and increase our wisdom is to recite the *Essence of Wisdom Sutra* with strong faith in Buddha while concentrating on its meaning. We should practise this method every day.

There is no more powerful remedy for overcoming hindrances and interferences than the practice of the perfection of wisdom as revealed in the *Essence of Wisdom Sutra*. There are many instances of sincere practitioners of the perfection of wisdom using this Sutra to avert harm and hindrances.

There was once a time when the god Indra was in danger of losing his life because of an attack by the powerful forces of jealous demi-gods. Indra had previously received teachings from Buddha and knew that to kill the demi-gods would be a serious transgression of those teachings. Wishing therefore to overcome his attackers by a peaceful method, Indra contemplated the profound meaning of the *Essence of Wisdom Sutra* while reciting its words. Through the power of his contemplation and recitation the demi-gods ceased their attack. Their anger subsided and their minds became peaceful and happy.

There are accounts of similar events taking place in Tibet. For example, there was once a very powerful practitioner of black magic called Kulo who brought great harm and even death to a large number of people in the area of Tibet where he lived. Fortunately at that time there lived nearby a pure Dharma practitioner called Lama Ukarwa. This Lama could not bear to allow the suffering inflicted by the wicked Kulo to continue unopposed, so one day he confronted the magician in the presence of a great crowd of people and said to him, 'It is true that you are a very powerful man, but if you continue your evil actions you will certainly be reborn in one of the lower realms and there you will have to experience great suffering. Therefore, it would be much better for you in the future if you gave up these harmful actions.' But Kulo, far from accepting this advice, became even more angry and uncontrolled. 'You are going to be the very next person I kill', he shouted, 'Before this week is over you will be dead as a result of my magic.'

He declared this before the frightened crowd and then stormed off, his mind consumed by hatred. All the people were very saddened by this. They were quite sure that within a week Lama Ukarwa would be dead because no one could withstand Kulo's magic. However, Ukarwa himself returned calmly to his home and began to practise a technique for averting harm that he had learned from a Kadampa master. This involved reciting and contemplating the *Essence of Wisdom Sutra*, which he did with great faith and concentration over the following days. Then, on the last day of the week, just as Kulo had predicted, there was a sudden death – but it was the magician himself and not Ukarwa who had died!

The people were amazed at this unexpected turn of events and thought that perhaps the Lama had also practised black magic. They came to him and asked whether this was true. Ukarwa replied that he had not done anything to kill or even to harm the magician, explaining that he had no such power and certainly no such intention. He told them that he had practised a technique to avert hindrances and as a result Kulo's magic had been neutralized. He suggested that perhaps Kulo's own evil powers had turned against him and caused his death. Ukarwa emphasized that he had had no intention to kill the magician.

Inspired by these events, the people requested teachings on the *Essence of Wisdom Sutra* and also received instruction on how to avert dangers using the Sutra. Many of them received signs indicating that their practice was successful, and thus they gained protection from various hindrances.

As a result of occurrences such as this the practices to avert hindrances using this Sutra became very popular in Tibet. There are many people who have direct personal experience of how effective these practices can be. For example, in 1954, Shigatse, the second largest city in Tibet, was in great danger of being flooded. After many houses had been destroyed the local people requested the monks of nearby Tashi Lhunpo Monastery to help avert the disaster. The monks left their monastery and assembled facing the approaching flood waters. First they recited the *Essence of Wisdom Sutra* and then they repeated the mantra of the perfection of wisdom many times, clapping their hands as indicated in the practice. As they did this the waters receded and the danger was averted, to the great relief of the people of the city.

Many Tibetans have experience of the great benefits of these practices. Very often if a family member becomes ill a Lama will be invited to their house to recite the Sutra and perform other rituals. I myself have participated in such practices and have seen personally how effective they can be.

As mentioned above, at one point during the practice to avert hindrances we clap our hands. The purpose of this is to remind us of emptiness. In many texts, it is stated that it is easier to develop an understanding of emptiness through contemplating sound than through contemplating other external objects such as visual form. When we clap our hands we can think, 'Where is the sound? Is it on the right hand? On the left hand? Somewhere in between? Or perhaps somewhere else?' If we check like this we cannot find the sound. Realizing that the sound cannot be found leads us to an understanding of emptiness.

An example of teaching emptiness using sound as the basis is found in the last chapters of the *Perfection of Wisdom Sutra in Eight Thousand Lines*. There a story is told about the great Teacher Dharmodgata who reveals the profound view of emptiness to the Bodhisattva Sadaprarudita by taking the sound of a lute as an example. It may be helpful to give a brief summary of this story.

Sadaprarudita was given this name, which means 'the one who is always crying', because he was filled with grief having searched unsuccessfully for a qualified Teacher who could reveal the perfection of wisdom. He would not give up his search, however, and asked everyone he met, 'Where is there a Teacher who can reveal to me the profound perfection of wisdom?'

One day, through the power of having purified the stains of previous non-virtuous actions, there appeared in the space before him a vision of a Buddha. The vision spoke to him, saying that he should travel east to a town called Gandhavati. There he would find the great Bodhisattva Dharmodgata who would give teachings on the perfection of wisdom. The vision then vanished. On hearing these words, Sadaprarudita was so joyful that he experienced a feeling of bliss similar to the blissful suppleness experienced by Yogis in deep meditation.

Sadaprarudita then reflected that he would like to bring a gift to Dharmodgata to express his respect and reverence for him. However, Sadaprarudita was poor and unable to buy even the smallest gift. Finally he thought, 'At the moment I am endowed with this human body of flesh and bone. If I do not make use of it now when will I be able to use it? If I sell portions of this body to others I will be able to buy worthy offerings for my Teacher, Dharmodgata.' Filled with a strong determination to sell his own body to fulfil his wish to make offerings, he travelled to a nearby town and stood in the market place calling out, 'Is there anyone here who would like to buy my body?' Despite his loud cries, no one seemed to hear him. Greatly disappointed, Sadaprarudita withdrew to one side and wept.

At that point, the chief of the gods, Indra, having seen what had happened, decided to test Sadaprarudita's resolve. In the guise of a high-caste Brahmin, he approached Sadaprarudita and said, 'Normally I have no use for human flesh but today there is a special ceremony for which I need a man's flesh, blood and marrow. I will pay you if you give these to me.'

Hearing this, Sadaprarudita was overjoyed. He immediately cut some flesh from his right thigh and drew to one side to smash his bone. The daughter of a local merchant living nearby witnessed this astonishing scene. Rushing outside, she asked Sadaprarudita why he was inflicting such treatment on himself. The Bodhisattva explained that he was selling his flesh to buy offerings so that he could honour the great Bodhisattva, Dharmodgata. The merchant's daughter asked why he wished to honour Dharmodgata and what benefits he hoped to receive. Sadaprarudita replied, 'Dharmodgata will explain to me the perfection of wisdom and skilful means. Through training in these I will attain great enlightenment and share the precious Dharma with all living beings.' When he explained the excellent qualities of Buddhahood the young woman developed great respect for the Three Jewels. She implored Sadaprarudita not to harm himself further and declared, 'I will give you whatever you require to honour Dharmodgata and I will come with you to him.'

Indra then threw off his disguise and stood before Sadaprarudita in his normal form. He proclaimed to the Bodhisattva, 'All the Buddhas of the past attained enlightenment through having just such a desire for Dharma as you have. I have no need of your flesh, I came here only to test you. Now choose whatever you want and I will give it to you.'

Sadaprarudita answered, 'Give me the supreme qualities of a Buddha!' Indra explained that such a request lay only within the province of the Buddhas; it was not within his power to grant. Sadaprarudita told Indra that he required no other wish to be granted and explained that he was able to heal his mutilated body through his special powers of declaring the truth. By these means his body was restored to its former whole state.

The story continues with an account of how Sadaprarudita finally met with Dharmodgata and made offerings to him. One of the first questions Sadaprarudita asked concerned the vision of a Buddha who had appeared and spoken to him. He asked Dharmodgata, 'Where did this Buddha come from and where did he go?'

Dharmodgata replied, 'Buddhas do not come from anywhere, nor do they go anywhere. Since Buddhas lack inherent existence they are completely empty.' It was then that Dharmodgata used the example of the sound of a lute to illustrate his point. He asked Sadaprarudita, 'Where does the sound of a lute come from and where does it go? Does it come from the strings, from within the lute, from the fingers of the player, from his effort to play, or from elsewhere? And when the sound has stopped, where does it go?'

In this way, Dharmodgata explained that, although Buddhas are empty of inherent existence they appear in dependence upon many causes and conditions, and when these causes and conditions cease Buddhas no longer appear. In this respect, Buddhas are like the sound of a lute. If we try to find the sound upon the strings of the lute or upon the fingers of the player and so forth we are unable to find it. This is because the sound is empty of inherent existence. Nevertheless, when all the appropriate causes and conditions are assembled, the sound of a lute will be produced, and when those causes and conditions cease the sound stops.

After Dharmodgata's explanation of the non-coming and non-going of Buddhas, using the illustration of the sound of a lute, the whole earth shook and many thousands of beings gained profound realizations of emptiness. Finally, through Dharmodgata's teachings on the perfection of wisdom, Sadaprarudita attained extraordinary concentrations on emptiness and many miracle powers.

The reason for recounting this story here is to illustrate that sound can be a very helpful basis for realizing emptiness. Thus, during the practice for averting hindrances that is explained next, we clap our hands four times to strengthen our recollection of emptiness. The story of Sadaprarudita also illustrates that in the past sincere practitioners were prepared to make determined efforts and undergo great hardships to receive teachings on the perfection of wisdom. They were happy to do this because they understood the great benefits of achieving and completing the perfection of wisdom.

THE ACTUAL PRACTICE TO OVERCOME HINDRANCES

I will now explain the practice *The Great Mother* presented in Appendix V, which includes the recitation and contemplation of the *Essence of Wisdom Sutra* that can be used to avert or overcome hindrances and obstacles. This practice can be used to overcome both the hindrances that afflict oneself and those afflicting others, and can also be directed towards overcoming both internal and external obstacles. The extent to which we are successful in overcoming obstacles through this practice, however, depends on the strength of our faith.

We begin this practice by visualizing the objects of refuge. In the space in front of us we visualize an extensive jewelled throne supported by eight snow lions. In the centre of this throne is a lotus flower, upon which is a moon seat (a circular cushion of white light) and a sun seat (a circular cushion of yellow light). Seated on the sun seat is the founder of the teachings, Buddha Shakyamuni, in his usual posture – his left hand rests in his lap holding a bowl, his right hand is in the earth-touching mudra, and his legs are crossed in the vajra posture. His body has the nature of golden light and he wears the robes of a fully ordained monk.

At Buddha Shakyamuni's heart, we visualize another lotus, moon and sun seat. On this is seated Great Mother Prajnaparamita, who is the embodiment of the Wisdom Truth Body of all the Buddhas. She has a body of golden light with one face and four arms. Her first right hand holds a golden vajra with nine prongs at each end, and her first left hand holds the *Perfection of Wisdom Sutra*. Her remaining two hands rest in her lap in the mudra of meditative equipoise. She is seated in the vajra posture, adorned with precious jewels and ornaments, and she wears beautiful garments of thin, heavenly material. We visualize Buddha Shakyamuni and the Great Mother as alive and real.

On the extensive throne, surrounding the two principal objects of refuge, are all the Buddhas and Bodhisattvas of the ten directions. In this way we visualize a vast assembly of refuge objects in the space before us. Without forgetting this visualization we begin reciting the practice.

First we recite three times the verses of going for refuge and generating bodhichitta. While we recite the first verse we remember the fears that face ourself and others, and with great faith go for refuge to the Three Jewels. While we recite the second verse we generate bodhichitta, the mind wishing to attain Buddhahood for the benefit of all living beings.

We then recite the third verse three times. During this recitation we focus our mind on the visualized objects of refuge and prostrate to them, make offerings and go for refuge. Finally we request their blessings. Here, when making prostrations, it is sufficient to place our hands together at our heart and generate a mind of respect and faith. We can make actual offerings of fresh water, flowers and so forth, or just visualize beautiful offerings being made.

Having completed these preliminaries we recite the text of the *Essence of Wisdom Sutra*. During this recitation we should maintain our faith and devotion towards the assembly of refuge objects and also contemplate the meaning of the Sutra.

When we have finished reciting the Sutra we turn our attention to the heart of Prajnaparamita. There, standing at the centre of a white moon cushion, is a blue letter HUM marked by a letter AH. We can visualize this as the Tibetan (see page 258) or Sanskrit letter, or as the English syllable. Surrounding the letter HUM, around the edge of the moon cushion, stand the letters of the perfection of wisdom mantra in a clockwise direction. The letters of the mantra are made of golden light but have the nature of the wisdom of Prajnaparamita herself. As we concentrate on these letters we remember the profound meaning of emptiness and recite the mantra. While reciting the mantra of the perfection of wisdom we contemplate that we, and all that offends and harms us, are empty of inherent existence. We recite the mantra as many times as is comfortable.

After the mantra recitation, we make requests to avert hindrances. While we recite the requesting verses we think about the harms and hindrances that we wish to overcome. When we reach the point where we recite:

> May all the harm of maras, non-humans and so forth
> be overcome

we clap our hands and imagine that the harms and hindrances gather into emptiness. Then, when we recite:

> May they become non-existent

we clap again and imagine that they dissolve into emptiness. When we recite:

> May they be pacified

we clap and imagine that they cease completely in emptiness. Finally, when we recite:

> May they be thoroughly pacified

we clap for the fourth time and think that none of the harms and hindrances can ever arise again.

As explained earlier, we clap our hands each time to remember emptiness. There are other similar practices in which we clap our hands three or nine times. Each system has its own significance and suitability.

We then meditate on emptiness of ourself and others. We can think that we, all that harms us, and the harm itself are all empty of inherent existence. We try to generate this realization and maintain it as well as we can. After the meditation on emptiness we recite the dedication verse.

If we wish to use this practice to overcome the four maras that afflict ourself and others there is a particular visualization that we can do during the part of the practice where we make requests to avert hindrances. We recall the harm and suffering experienced by all living beings as a result of the mara of the delusions and the other maras, and, using this as a basis, generate the mind of great compassion and a strong wish to free all living beings from the four maras.

For the purpose of this practice we visualize the four maras in physical form. We visualize the mara of the delusions as a host of yellow human beings riding yellow horses. Each rider holds a metal sword in his right hand and a noose in his left. It is important to remember that in essence these horsemen are delusions – the delusions are merely appearing in this aspect. Because the delusions that afflict living beings are beyond measure we visualize these horsemen filling the whole of space.

The visualizations of the other three maras are very similar, differing only in the colour of the horses and riders and the weapons carried. In the case of the mara of the aggregates, the horses and riders are red and each rider carries a spear and a noose. The mara of the Lord of Death appears as black horsemen riding black horses, with each rider holding a wooden sword and a noose. Lastly, we visualize the Devaputra maras as white horsemen on white horses, with each rider holding a white flower and a noose.

When we clap our hands the first time we imagine that all the yellow horsemen, who in essence are delusions, gather and dissolve into emptiness, become non-existent, and will never arise again, like a rainbow dissolving into the sky without leaving a trace. We then think that we have accomplished our wish to free all living beings from delusions. Then, when we clap our hands the second time we imagine that the red horsemen, who in essence are the contaminated aggregates of all living beings, gather and dissolve into emptiness, become non-existent, and will never arise again. Similarly, when we clap our hands the third time we destroy the black horsemen who in essence are the mara of the Lord of Death, and when we clap our hands the fourth time we destroy the white horsemen who in essence are the Devaputra maras. When we have completed this practice, we think, 'I have now freed all living beings from the four maras!', and we generate a feeling of great joy.

This practice is an excellent method for developing great compassion and bodhichitta as well as for developing wisdom realizing emptiness. When we eventually attain Buddhahood through completing the spiritual paths of method and wisdom we will actually have the ability to help others overcome the four maras. The practice described here takes the future result, Buddhahood, and uses it in the path right now. By imaginirg that we already have abilities that we wish to gain in the future we create the cause to attain them more quickly.

Finally, it should be mentioned that these practices to avert hindrances can be done in either a peaceful or a wrathful manner. The method described here is the peaceful method. Those who have received an empowerment into Highest Yoga Tantra may do these practices in a powerful, wrathful manner. However, whichever way we do these practices we should be mindful of the underlying meaning of what we are doing. Simply clapping our hands has no great meaning. To attain true freedom from obstacles and accomplish the full awakening of Buddhahood it is necessary to gain experience of the actual perfection of wisdom.

Colophon: This explanation of the sadhana or ritual prayer for spiritual attainments of Great Mother Prajnaparamita was composed by Venerable Geshe Kelsang Gyatso based on traditional sources.

Appendix VII

The Yoga of Great Mother
Prajnaparamita:
Self-generation sadhana

The Yoga of Great Mother Prajnaparamita:
Self-generation sadhana

INTRODUCTION

When we receive the blessing empowerment of Great Mother Prajnaparamita we receive the instructions on training in common paths and training in uncommon paths, and we receive special blessings. To make these instructions effective we need to engage in the practice of the yoga of Great Mother Prajnaparamita self-generation sadhana.

Great Mother Prajnaparamita is a female Buddha who is the manifestation of Buddha's perfection of wisdom. Her function is to overcome maras – the outer and inner obstructing demons – and to bestow the realization of the higher perfection of wisdom. Buddha's perfection of wisdom appears as the wisdom being, Prajnaparamita. She has a body of golden light with one face and four arms. Her four arms indicate that she is the synthesis of all Buddhas of the four directions. She holds a vajra and a scripture of the *Perfection of Wisdom Sutra* indicating that she bestows upon us the attainment of the union of great bliss and emptiness, which is the higher perfection of wisdom. Her other two hands rest in her lap in the mudra of meditative equipoise. This mudra teaches us that through training in meditation on the perfection of wisdom we can accomplish the higher perfection of wisdom, the union of great bliss and emptiness, through which we can attain enlightenment very quickly.

Wisdom is a virtuous intelligent mind whose function is to dispel the inner darkness of ignorance. With wisdom we can understand how things really are. Normally we do not understand the real nature of things. This is ignorance. Moreover, we do not understand that suffering comes from non-virtuous actions and happiness from virtuous actions. This too is ignorance. Because of this ignorance, even though we do not want to suffer we create our own suffering by performing non-virtuous actions. And although we want to be happy all the time we destroy our own happiness by developing anger, negative views and wrong intentions. We should know that this is our normal situation.

All our suffering and problems come from our ignorance. Because of ignorance we have experienced suffering and problems in life after life, from beginningless time until now. Now is the time to abandon ignorance permanently because we have a precious human life and have met Buddhadharma. The only method to abandon our ignorance and attain the supreme happiness of enlightenment is to accomplish the perfection of wisdom in general, and especially the higher perfection of wisdom.

Wisdom that is motivated by the supreme good heart, bodhichitta, is the perfection of wisdom, and wisdom that is the union of great bliss and emptiness, the quick path to enlightenment, is the higher perfection of wisdom. Through sincere practice of the yoga of Great Mother Prajnaparamita we can accomplish these wisdoms, have the ability to gain victory over maras – the outer and inner obstructing demons – and become an enlightened being like Buddha Shakyamuni. How wonderful!

In summary, while we have this human life and have met Buddhadharma, we should apply great effort to entering the profound path of the perfection of wisdom and making progress along this path, from the path of accumulation to the Path of No More Learning.

Geshe Kelsang Gyatso
2008

Great Mother Prajnaparamita

The Yoga of Great Mother Prajnaparamita

ACCOMPLISHING THE SELF-GENERATION

PRELIMINARIES

Going for refuge and promising to accomplish a Buddha's enlightenment to benefit all mother beings

In this practice we should think:

I can permanently protect and liberate myself and others from suffering only by putting Dharma into practice, receiving Buddha's blessings and receiving help and support from Sangha – the supreme spiritual friends. Therefore I will make the promise to rely sincerely upon the Three Jewels – Buddha, Dharma and Sangha – throughout my life and to accomplish a Buddha's enlightenment.

Thinking in this way we take refuge vows and Bodhisattva vows by reciting the following ritual prayer three times.

I go for refuge to the Three Jewels – Buddha, Dharma and
    Sangha,
And confess individually all negative actions.

I rejoice in the virtues of all beings
And promise to accomplish a Buddha's enlightenment. (3x)

Guru yoga

VISUALIZATION

In the space before me is Guru Buddha Shakyamuni
surrounded by all the Buddhas and Bodhisattvas, like the
full moon surrounded by stars. At his heart is the Great
Mother Prajnaparamita, the manifestation of Buddha's
perfection of wisdom.

**PROSTRATION, OFFERING, CONFESSION, REJOICING, BESEECHING,
REQUESTING AND DEDICATION**

However many Lions of Conqueror Buddhas there are
In the worlds of the ten directions and three times,
To all of them without exception
I prostrate with body, speech and mind.

By the power of my excellent pure view,
All Conqueror Buddhas appear clearly to my mind;
Bowing with bodies numerous as atoms of the world,
I prostrate to all these Conqueror Buddhas.

Upon each atom are Buddhas numerous as atoms,
Surrounded by all Bodhisattvas;
In this way I visualize the Conqueror Buddhas
Filling the ground and all of space.

With an inexhaustible chorus of praise
And the sound of infinite prayer,
I proclaim the good qualities of all the Buddhas
And praise all Those Gone to Bliss.

For all the Buddhas I visualize
A vast array of unsurpassed offerings.
By the power of my faith in their excellent deeds,
I prostrate and make offerings to them all.

Whatever negative actions I have done
With my body, speech and mind,
Whether out of attachment, hatred or confusion,
I confess every single one.

I rejoice in all the merits
Of the Buddhas of the ten directions,
Bodhisattvas, Solitary Conquerors, Hearer Learners,
Hearer No-More-Learners and all living beings.

You who are lamps for the worlds of the ten directions,
Protectors of all living beings,
Who have attained the ultimate state of Buddhahood,
I beseech you to turn the unsurpassed Wheel of Dharma.

With my palms pressed together, I make this request
To all those who wish to display passing away:
Please remain for as many aeons as there are atoms in the
    world,
To bring benefit and happiness to all living beings.

All the merit I have accumulated
By prostrating, offering, making confession,
Rejoicing, beseeching and requesting,
I dedicate to great enlightenment.

OFFERING THE MANDALA

The ground sprinkled with perfume and spread with
    flowers,
The Great Mountain, four lands, sun and moon,
Seen as a Buddha Land and offered thus,
May all beings enjoy such Pure Lands.

I offer without any sense of loss
The objects that give rise to my attachment, hatred and
    confusion,
My friends, enemies and strangers, our bodies and
    enjoyments;
Please accept these and bless me to be released directly
    from the three poisons.

IDAM GURU RATNA MANDALAKAM NIRYATAYAMI

MAKING REQUESTS

O Blessed One Shakyamuni Buddha,
Great Mother Prajnaparamita,
And all Buddhas of the ten directions,
To you I prostrate, make offerings and go for refuge.
Please bless my mental continuum.   (3x)

RECEIVING BLESSINGS AND PURIFYING

Through my making sincere requests in this way, infinite
rays of blue, yellow, white, red and green wisdom light
radiate from Buddha Shakyamuni's body, filling my entire
body from the crown of my head to the soles of my feet.
All my outer and inner obstacles, especially my ordinary
appearance of body, speech and mind, are purified.

ACTUAL SELF-GENERATION

With delight all the holy beings dissolve into Buddha Shakyamuni. He dissolves into Great Mother Prajnaparamita at his heart and she in turn dissolves into me. My body transforms into yellow light, becoming smaller and smaller from above and below until finally it dissolves into the emptiness of all phenomena, the mere absence of all the things that I normally see.

In the vast space of emptiness of all phenomena appears Akanishta Pure Land, where I appear as Great Mother Prajnaparamita. I have a golden-coloured body of wisdom light with one face and four arms. My first right hand holds a golden vajra and my first left hand holds a scripture of the *Perfection of Wisdom Sutra*. My remaining two hands rest in my lap in the mudra of meditative equipoise. I sit in the vajra posture adorned with precious jewelled ornaments and wear beautiful garments of heavenly silk. Although I have this appearance it is not other than the emptiness of all phenomena.

At this point we should emphasize meditation on ourself as Great Mother Prajnaparamita in our Pure Land of Akanishta while realizing that this appearance is not other than the emptiness of all phenomena. This meditation is called the 'yoga of non-dual profundity and clarity' and is very profound.

Reciting the mantra

While maintaining the recognition that Wisdom Being Prajnaparamita is at our heart, we recite the following mantra requesting her to bestow upon us the realization of the higher perfection of wisdom and to help us to overcome maras.

OM AH PRAJNAPARAMITA HUM HUM PHAT   (21x, 100x, etc.)

TAYATHA OM GATE GATE PARAGATE PARASAMGATE BODHI
SÖHA   (7x, 21x, etc.)

The meaning of the mantra OM AH PRAJNAPARAMITA HUM HUM PHAT is: OM is symbolic of the bodies of all Buddhas, AH is symbolic of the speech of all Buddhas, the first HUM is symbolic of the mind of all Buddhas, PRAJNAPARAMITA means we are calling her, the second HUM requests her to bestow attainments of the higher perfection of wisdom and PHAT requests her to pacify obstacles. Altogether the meaning is: 'O Great Mother Prajnaparamita, synthesis of all Buddhas' body, speech and mind, please bestow attainments and pacify obstacles'.

The meaning of the mantra TAYATHA OM GATE GATE PARAGATE PARASAMGATE BODHI SÖHA is: OM we are calling the Great Mother Prajnaparamita, SÖHA requests her to bestow the five attainments, which are (1) the perfection of wisdom of initial realization, revealed by the first GATE, (2) the perfection of wisdom of superior seeing, revealed by the second GATE, (3) the perfection of wisdom of the path of seeing, revealed by PARAGATE, (4) the perfection of wisdom of the path of meditation, revealed by PARASAMGATE, and (5) the perfection of wisdom of enlightenment, revealed by BODHI.

In the Heart Sutra *these five wisdoms are also called respectively: the mantra of the perfection of wisdom, the mantra of great knowledge, the unsurpassed mantra, the equal-to-the-unequalled mantra, and the mantra that thoroughly pacifies all suffering.*

'Mantra' means inner protection. An actual mantra is a wisdom realization that directly protects living beings from suffering, and mantras that we verbally recite are methods to accomplish the actual mantra.

Dedication

Through my virtues from engaging
In the profound practice of Prajnaparamita,
May I accomplish a Buddha's enlightenment
To liberate all mother living beings.

May the maras – the outer and inner obstructing demons –
Be quickly and completely pacified,
And may all living beings swiftly become
Conqueror Buddhas like Shakyamuni Buddha.

May Buddhadharma, the sole medicine for all suffering,
And the source of all happiness,
Be materially supported and honoured,
And remain for a very long time.

Prayers for the Virtuous Tradition

So that the tradition of Je Tsongkhapa,
The King of the Dharma, may flourish,
May all obstacles be pacified
And may all favourable conditions abound.

Through the two collections of myself and others
Gathered throughout the three times,
May the doctrine of Conqueror Losang Dragpa
Flourish for evermore.

The nine-line *Migtsema* prayer

Tsongkhapa, crown ornament of the scholars of the Land
of the Snows,
You are Buddha Shakyamuni and Vajradhara, the source
of all attainments,
Avalokiteshvara, the treasury of unobservable compassion,
Manjushri, the supreme stainless wisdom,
And Vajrapani, the destroyer of the hosts of maras.
O Venerable Guru-Buddha, synthesis of all Three Jewels,
With my body, speech and mind, respectfully I make
requests:
Please grant your blessings to ripen and liberate myself and
others,
And bestow the common and supreme attainments.   (3x)

Colophon: This sadhana or ritual prayer for spiritual
attainments of Great Mother Prajnaparamita was
compiled by Venerable Geshe Kelsang Gyatso
based on traditional sources, January 2008

Appendix VIII

A Short Commentary to
*The Yoga of Great Mother
Prajnaparamita:*
Self-generation Sadhana

Appendix VII

A Short Commentary to
The Yoga of Great Mother Prajnaparamita:
Self-generation Sadhana

This commentary has been prepared for those who have received the empowerment of Great Mother Prajnaparamita. It is based on the sadhana or 'ritual prayer for spiritual attainments' called *The Yoga of Great Mother Prajnaparamita* found in Appendix VII. In this context, 'yoga' means 'training in spiritual paths'. This yoga is a training in spiritual paths that leads us to the attainment of Great Mother Prajnaparamita. Through this training we can control the inner obstructing demons of our delusions, especially our self-grasping and self-cherishing, and thus maintain a peaceful mind all the time and always be happy. We will also develop higher and higher levels of wisdom, ultimately attain enlightenment, and thus be able to benefit each and every living being directly every day. Understanding these benefits we should encourage ourself to engage sincerely in this yoga practice.

This practice has two stages: training in preliminary practices, and training in the actual practice of self-generation.

TRAINING IN PRELIMINARY PRACTICES

In this yoga, we engage in three preliminary practices: going for refuge, generating the supreme good heart of bodhichitta – promising to accomplish a Buddha's enlightenment to benefit all mother beings – and Guru yoga.

As indicated in the sadhana, we begin the practices of going for refuge and generating bodhichitta by thinking we can permanently protect and liberate ourself and others from suffering only by putting Dharma into practice, receiving Buddha's blessings and receiving help and support from Sangha – the supreme spiritual friends including our Spiritual Teacher. We therefore make the promise to rely sincerely upon the Three Jewels – Buddha, Dharma and Sangha – throughout our life and to accomplish a Buddha's enlightenment. Thinking in this way we take refuge vows and Bodhisattva vows by reciting three times, from the depths of our heart, the ritual four-line prayer in the sadhana, while contemplating its meaning.

This four-line prayer is extracted from Tantric scriptures composed by Buddha Vajradhara and is used by Tantric practitioners to take Bodhisattva vows. Although it has only four lines it is very special and has deep meaning. It can be interpreted in many ways according to different levels of understanding. I will now explain its definitive meaning according to Vajradhara's main intention.

When we recite, either mentally or verbally, the first line, 'I go for refuge to the Three Jewels – Buddha, Dharma and Sangha', we are promising to go for refuge to Buddha, Dharma and Sangha throughout our life. This promise is the refuge vow, and is the basic foundation for training in the Bodhisattva's way of life. With the second line,

'And confess individually all negative actions', we are promising to train in the Bodhisattva's moral discipline of refraining from non-virtue, or moral discipline of restraint. We are also promising to apply effort to purifying all our non-virtues and downfalls together with their causes, the delusions, which are the main obstacles to the practice of the Bodhisattva vows. With the third line, 'I rejoice in the virtues of all beings', we are promising to train in the Bodhisattva's moral discipline of gathering virtuous actions or Dharmas. Rejoicing in the virtues of others is the best way to engage in virtue. The words 'the virtues of all beings' can also refer to the six perfections; 'all beings' in this context referring to 'all Bodhisattvas', and 'I rejoice in' meaning 'I will engage in'. Because every living being needs to attain permanent liberation from suffering and enlightenment, they need to follow the path to enlightenment – the Bodhisattva path – which is the practice of the six perfections. The third line can therefore refer to our determination to engage in the Bodhisattva's path by practising the six perfections. With the fourth line we are promising to train in the Bodhisattva's moral discipline of benefitting living beings. When we say, 'I promise to accomplish a Buddha's enlightenment', we are promising to benefit all living beings by attaining enlightenment. This promise is the actual Bodhisattva vow; by making this promise we are generating actual bodhichitta.

'Guru' is a Sanskrit word meaning Spiritual Guide. Our Spiritual Guide is anyone who sincerely leads us to correct spiritual paths – spiritual trainings that lead us to a state of pure happiness – by giving teachings and showing a good example. Guru yoga is a special way of training in relying upon our Spiritual Guide.

We begin this Guru yoga practice by visualizing in the space before us our Spiritual Guide in the aspect of Buddha Shakyamuni surrounded by all the Buddhas and Bodhisattvas, like the full moon surrounded by stars. At his heart is Great Mother Prajnaparamita, the manifestation of Buddha's perfection of wisdom. Buddha Shakyamuni and Prajnaparamita are not two different beings; it is Buddha's own heart that appears as Prajnaparamita. We meditate, at least for a short while, on this visualization without distraction.

The purpose of visualizing our Spiritual Guide in the aspect of Buddha Shakyamuni is to prevent our seeing him or her as an ordinary person. While meditating on this visualization we should remember that we are visualizing Guru Buddha Shakyamuni – Buddha Shakyamuni inseparably one with our Spiritual Guide – and develop deep faith.

While holding this visualization we should emphasize three things. The first is remembering the meaning of Buddha's words when he said, 'In future degenerate times I will appear as ordinary Spiritual Teachers. You should know that I am these Teachers.' We should strongly believe that our Spiritual Guide who sincerely leads us to correct spiritual paths is an emanation of Buddha Shakyamuni, and continually meditate on this belief single-pointedly until we hold it spontaneously. This belief is the root of Dharma realizations, the actual spiritual path to liberation and enlightenment.

Second, while believing that our Spiritual Guide is an emanation of Buddha Shakyamuni we emphasize engaging sincerely in the practices of the seven limbs – the practices of prostration, offering, confession or purification, rejoicing, beseeching, requesting and dedication – and offering the mandala, every day with strong faith in Guru Buddha

Shakyamuni, together with reciting the verses from the sadhana. These are powerful methods for accumulating merit, virtue or good fortune, purifying negativities and receiving blessings. More detail on these practices can be found in the book *Joyful Path of Good Fortune*.

Third, we emphasize shining the sun of our faith continually on the snow mountain of our Spiritual Guide, Guru Buddha Shakyamuni, and making strong requests for him to bestow upon us blessings to attain realizations of common and uncommon spiritual paths, while reciting three times the request prayer from the sadhana. In response to our requests the blessing waters of all the Buddhas of the ten directions will flow into our mind. We imagine infinite rays of blue, yellow, white, red, and green wisdom light radiate from Guru Buddha Shakyamuni's body and fill our entire body from the crown of our head to the soles of our feet. All our outer and inner obstacles – especially our ordinary appearance of body, speech and mind – are purified and our very subtle body receives a special power to transform into the divine illusory body, which is the deathless body, and our very subtle mind receives a special power to transform into the higher perfection of wisdom, the union of great bliss and emptiness.

If we emphasize these three things we can attain full enlightenment very quickly. However, the effectiveness of our Guru yoga practice depends on the strength of our belief in karma. If it is weak we will neglect to engage in practices for accumulating merit, purifying our negativities and receiving Buddha's blessings, and then our Guru yoga practice will be just empty words.

TRAINING IN THE ACTUAL PRACTICE
OF SELF-GENERATION

Self-generation means generating ourself as an enlightened being and our world as an enlightened world. In this practice we generate as Great Mother Prajnaparamita and our world as the Pure Land of Akanishta. Training in self-generation is a quick method to transform ourself into an enlightened being, a completely pure being. The effectiveness of this training depends on understanding that our self that we normally see does not exist. If it did exist it would be impossible to generate ourself as an enlightened being, because it is impossible for one person to be both a deluded being and an enlightened being who has no delusions.

Therefore, to generate ourself as an enlightened Buddha such as Great Mother Prajnaparamita we should first know clearly that our self that we normally see does not exist. Normally, we point at our body or mind and say, 'This is me', but this is wrong. Our body is not our self – in reality our body originally came from our parents – and our mind is not our self. We say, 'My body and my mind', indicating that our body and mind are possessed by our self; and a possessor cannot be the same as its possessions. However, there is no 'our self' other than our body and mind. If we were to imagine our body and mind disappearing there would be nothing left that we could call 'our self'. Through searching in this way we will realize that our self that we normally see does not exist and we will perceive the mere absence of our self that we normally see, the emptiness of our self. We then meditate on this emptiness single-pointedly for as long as possible. In the same way, we meditate on the emptiness of all phenomena. Gradually, our mistaken appearance of perceiving an inherently existent self and world will cease, and we will have no problem in transforming ourself into an enlightened being and our world into a Pure Land. We should remember the teachings on emptiness explained earlier in this book, and integrate our understanding of these teachings into our practice of self-generation.

We should train every day in both meditation on the emptiness of all phenomena and self-generation using the sadhana practice. With deep experience of meditation on emptiness, our self-generation practice will be very effective and quickly bring successful results.

Following the sadhana, we begin our training in self-generation by imagining that all the holy beings, the Buddhas and Bodhisattvas, surrounding Guru Buddha Shakyamuni dissolve into him. He dissolves into Great Mother Prajnaparamita at his heart and she in turn dissolves into us. Our body transforms into golden-yellow light, which becomes smaller and smaller from above and below until finally it dissolves into the emptiness of all phenomena, the mere absence of all the things that we normally see. At this point we perceive only emptiness, and we meditate on emptiness single-pointedly at least for a short while.

Then, within the state of emptiness, we generate ourself as a new being, a pure enlightened being, Great Mother Prajnaparamita, in Akanishta Pure Land. We then meditate on the appearance of our body, the body of Great Mother Prajnaparamita, while realizing that this appearance is not other than the emptiness of all phenomena.

We have a body of yellow light, which in nature is wisdom. We have one face and four arms. Our four arms indicate that as the self-generated Prajnaparamita we are the synthesis of all the Buddhas of the four directions. Our first right hand holds a golden nine-pronged vajra, which symbolizes our purified five aggregates – the basis for imputing ourself as Prajnaparamita – and purified four elements of earth, water, fire and wind. Our first left hand holds a scripture, which is the *Perfection of Wisdom Sutra*, indicating that as Great Mother Prajnaparamita we can bestow the attainment of the union of great bliss and emptiness upon all beings, and that to attain this realization of the higher perfection of wisdom all living beings must listen to, understand and practise the perfection of wisdom that Buddha explained in the *Perfection of Wisdom Sutra*. Our other two hands rest in our lap in the mudra of meditative equipoise, indicating that through training in meditation on the higher perfection of wisdom all living beings can attain enlightenment very quickly. We sit in the vajra posture, adorned with precious jewelled ornaments and wear beautiful garments of heavenly silk.

At first we generate ourself as the enlightened Buddha Great Mother Prajnaparamita mainly through the power of our concentration and correct belief, which is the nature of wisdom. When we begin the practice of self-generation we do not need to think in detail about our colour, shape and so forth; we should simply believe that in the vast space of emptiness – the cessation of our grasping at things that we normally see – appears Akanishta Pure Land in which we appear as Prajnaparamita. We need to contemplate and meditate on this self-generation again and again until we spontaneously believe that we are Prajnaparamita in our Pure Land. Eventually, when we develop deep familiarity with this, the ordinary appearance of our body and all other things will naturally cease completely, and the appearance of ourself as Great Mother Prajnaparamita in Akanishta will spontaneously arise. When this happens we will experience the supreme happiness of enlightenment.

It is important to meditate on the appearance of this self-generation while realizing that it is not other than the emptiness of all phenomena. Our one mind of concentration simultaneously meditates on two things: the self-generated appearance of ourself as Prajnaparamita, and the realization that this appearance is not other than the emptiness of all phenomena. This meditation is called the 'yoga of non-dual profundity and clarity' – the non-dual union of appearance and emptiness. It is very subtle, profound and the real quick path to enlightenment.

In this context, 'clarity' means the mere appearance of ourself as Prajnaparamita and our world as Akanishta, which is subtle conventional truth. 'Profundity' refers to the mere absence of all the things that we normally see, which is ultimate truth. These two truths – mere appearance and emptiness – are non-dual, which means they are one object, or entity, with different names, one called 'appearance' and the other 'emptiness'. At this point we should integrate our understanding of the four profundities, especially the profundities of the union of the two truths and the nominal distinction of the two truths, explained earlier in this book. When, through continually practising the meditation on self-generation, we realize that the appearance of ourself as Prajnaparamita in Akanishta Pure Land is emptiness we have realized non-dual profundity and clarity. Initially we will realize non-dual profundity and clarity with a conceptual mind, but eventually we will realize this directly with a very subtle non-conceptual mind of great bliss.

This one single concentration or meditation on non-dual profundity and clarity accumulates both a great collection of merit, the cause of attaining Buddha's Form Body or Rupakaya, and a great collection of wisdom, the cause of attaining Buddha's Truth Body or Dharmakaya. With deep experience of this meditation we do not need to engage in external actions to accumulate merit. Whatever we do, day and night, even during sleep, will accumulate both merit and wisdom.

While continuing to meditate on non-dual profundity and clarity, with a concentrated mind of correct belief we generate ourself as enlightened being Great Mother Prajnaparamita and our world as Akanishta Pure Land. When we perceive even a rough mental, or generic, image of ourself as Prajnaparamita and our world as Akanishta, we hold this without forgetting and remain on this generation single-pointedly. We should continually learn and train in this meditation many times every day.

This new generation of ourself as enlightened being Prajnaparamita and our world as Akanishta – without perceiving any other appearance – is the object of our meditation. We should improve our concentration on this object at first for just one or two minutes and then gradually increase this to five minutes. This is the first level of concentration, or mental abiding. Then, by continually improving and developing greater familiarity we can gradually progress through the nine levels of concentration, developing a concentration that is progressively purer, clearer and of longer duration. In this way we will improve our clarity, or clear appearance, and divine pride thinking, 'I am Prajnaparamita.' In this way, perceiving Prajnaparamita clearly, we can improve our concentration from lower to higher levels through the nine levels, as explained in books such as *Modern Buddhism, Joyful Path of Good Fortune* and *Meaningful to Behold.* Although the object of meditation is different in these books the development of concentration is the same. After the ninth level we will gain the concentration of tranquil abiding observing this new self-generation. Because our motivation is the compassionate mind of bodhichitta all these concentrations and wisdoms are Bodhisattva paths.

Although we initially appear as Prajnaparamita and we believe, 'I am Prajnaparamita in Akanishta Pure Land', this is imagined or created, like a rough sketch made by an artist before he completes the actual painting. Although this is created by our concentration and correct belief, we should always believe that the actual wisdom being Prajnaparamita is at our heart.

After meditating on the yoga of non-dual profundity and clarity we engage in mantra recitation. While maintaining the recognition that Wisdom Being Prajnaparamita is at our heart, we recite the following mantra requesting her to bestow upon us the realization of the higher perfection of wisdom and to help us to overcome maras. We first recite OM AH PRAJNAPARAMITA HUM HUM PHAT twenty-one times or more, and then we recite TAYATHA OM GATE GATE PARAGATE PARASAMGATE BODHI SÖHA twenty-one times or more. We can, if we wish, engage in a close retreat and collect either 10,000 or 100,000 or more of these mantras.

The meaning of the mantra OM AH PRAJNAPARAMITA HUM HUM PHAT is as follows. OM is symbolic of the bodies of all Buddhas, AH is symbolic of the speech of all Buddhas, the first HUM is symbolic of the mind of all Buddhas, PRAJNAPARAMITA means we are calling her, the second HUM requests her to bestow attainments of the higher perfection of wisdom and PHAT requests her to pacify obstacles. Altogether the meaning is: 'O Great Mother Prajnaparamita, synthesis of all Buddhas' body, speech and mind, please bestow attainments and pacify obstacles.' With this request we recite this mantra with deep faith.

The general meaning of the mantra TAYATHA OM GATE GATE PARAGATE PARASAMGATE BODHI SÖHA has already been explained in Part One. Specifically, in this context, with OM we are calling the Great Mother Prajnaparamita, SÖHA requests her to bestow the five attainments which are (1) the perfection of wisdom of initial realization – which means the perfection of wisdom that is the path of accumulation – revealed by the first GATE, (2) the perfection of wisdom of superior seeing – that is, the perfection of wisdom of the path of preparation – revealed by the second GATE, (3) the perfection of wisdom of the path of seeing, revealed by PARAGATE, (4) the perfection of wisdom of the path of meditation, revealed by PARASAMGATE, and (5) the perfection of wisdom of enlightenment revealed by BODHI. We are therefore requesting Prajnaparamita, 'Please bestow upon me these five different levels of wisdom; these are what I really need to make my human life meaningful.' We should request this from the depths of our heart.

We then finish each session by dedicating the merit purely and sincerely together with reciting the prayers from the sadhana.

This is a short but essential explanation of how to train in the self-generation practice of Great Mother Prajnaparamita. We can improve our understanding of generation stage and completion stage by reading books such as *Modern Buddhism*, *Mahamudra Tantra*, *Clear Light of Bliss* and *Guide to Dakini Land*.

Geshe Kelsang Gyatso
11th November 2011

Glossary

Akanishta A Pure Land where Bodhisattvas attain enlightenment. See *Clear Light of Bliss*.

Amitabha The manifestation of the speech of all Buddhas, and of their aggregate of discrimination. He has a red-coloured body. See *Eight Steps to Happiness*.

Amitayus A Buddha who increases our lifespan, merit and wisdom. He is the Enjoyment Body aspect of Buddha Amitabha.

Analytical meditation The mental process of investigating a virtuous object – analyzing its nature, function, characteristics and other aspects. See *Joyful Path of Good Fortune* and *The New Meditation Handbook*.

Aryadeva A third century AD Indian Buddhist scholar and meditation master, who was a disciple of Nagarjuna.

Atisha (AD 982-1054) A famous Indian Buddhist scholar and meditation master. He was Abbot of the great Buddhist monastery of Vikramashila at a time when Mahayana Buddhism was flourishing in India. He was later invited to Tibet where he reintroduced pure Buddhism. He is the author of the first text on the stages of the path (Lamrim), *Lamp for the Path*. His tradition later became known as the 'Kadampa Tradition'. See *Modern Buddhism* and *Joyful Path of Good Fortune*.

Beginningless time According to the Buddhist world view, there is no beginning to mind, and so no beginning to time. Therefore, all living beings have taken countless previous rebirths.

Blessing The transformation of our mind from a negative state to a positive state, from an unhappy state to a happy state, or from a state of weakness to a state of strength, through the inspiration of holy beings such as our Spiritual Guide, Buddhas and Bodhisattvas.

Bodh Gaya The place where Buddha Shakyamuni showed the manner of attaining enlightenment; near the modern city of Gaya in the north Indian state of Bihar.

Brahma A worldly god, who resides in the first form realm. See *Ocean of Nectar*.

Buddha nature The root mind of a sentient being, and its ultimate nature. Buddha seed, Buddha nature and Buddha lineage are synonyms. All sentient beings have Buddha nature and therefore have the potential to attain Buddhahood. See *Mahamudra Tantra*.

Buddha's bodies A Buddha has four bodies – the Wisdom Truth Body, the Nature Body, the Enjoyment Body and the Emanation Body. The first is Buddha's omniscient mind. The second is the emptiness, or ultimate nature, of his or her mind. The third is his subtle Form Body. The fourth, of which each Buddha manifests a countless number, are gross Form Bodies that are visible to ordinary beings. The Wisdom Truth Body and the Nature Body are both included within the Truth Body, and the Enjoyment Body and the Emanation Body are both included within the Form Body. See *Joyful Path of Good Fortune, Tantric Grounds and Paths* and *Ocean of Nectar*.

Chakravatin king An extremely fortunate being who has accumulated a vast amount of merit and as a result has taken rebirth as a king with dominion over all the four continents as described in Buddhist cosmology, or, at the very least, over one of the four continents. At present there are no chakravatin kings in our world, and there is no one who has complete dominion over our continent, Jambudipa. See *Great Treasury of Merit*.

Chandrakirti (circa 7th century AD) A great Indian Buddhist scholar and meditation master who composed, among many other books, the well-known *Guide to the Middle Way*, in which he clearly elucidates the view of the Madhyamika-Prasangika school according to Buddha's teachings given in the *Perfection of Wisdom Sutras*. See *Ocean of Nectar*.

Changkya Rolpai Dorje (AD 1717-1786) A famous Gelugpa Lama and tutor to the Chinese Emperor, who greatly influenced the development of Buddhism in China, Mongolia and Tibet.

Collection of merit A virtuous action motivated by bodhichitta that is a main cause of attaining the Form Body of a Buddha. Examples are: making offerings and prostrations to holy beings with bodhichitta motivation, and the practice of the perfections of giving, moral discipline and patience.

Collection of wisdom A virtuous mental action motivated by bodhichitta that is a main cause of attaining the Truth Body of a Buddha. Examples are: listening to, contemplating and meditating on emptiness with bodhichitta motivation.

Conceptual mind A thought that apprehends its object through a generic, or mental, image. See *Understanding the Mind*.

Dedication Dedication is by nature a virtuous mental factor; it is the virtuous intention that functions both to prevent accumulated virtue from degenerating and to cause its increase. See *Joyful Path of Good Fortune*.

Deluded doubt A two-pointedness of mind that interferes with the attainment of liberation or enlightenment. See *Understanding the Mind*.

Demi-god A being of the demi-god realm, the second highest of the six realms of samsara. Demi-gods are similar to gods but their bodies, possessions and environments are inferior. See *Joyful Path of Good Fortune*.

Desire realm The environment of hell beings, hungry spirits, animals, human beings, demi-gods and the gods who enjoy the five objects of desire.

Dharma Buddha's teachings and the inner realizations that are attained in dependence upon practising them. 'Dharma' means 'protection'. By practising Buddha's teachings, we protect ourself from suffering and problems.

Dharmakaya Sanskrit term for the Truth Body of a Buddha. See also *Buddha's bodies*.

Direct perceiver A cognizer that apprehends its manifest object. According to the lower Buddhist schools, a direct perceiver is necessarily non-conceptual, but according to the Madhyamika-Prasangikas, direct perceivers include the subsequent moments of an inferential, or subsequent, cognizer, which are conceptual minds. See *Understanding the Mind*.

Element (Tib. kham) The nature of any phenomenon. All phenomena hold their own natures, which are all included within the eighteen elements. See *Ocean of Nectar*.

Elements (Tib. jung wa) Earth, water, fire, wind, and space. All matter can be said to be composed of a combination of these elements. There are five inner elements (those that are conjoined with the continuum of a person), and five outer elements (those that are not conjoined with the continuum of a person). These elements are not the same as the earth of a field, the water of a river and so forth. Rather, the elements of earth, water, fire, wind and space in broad terms are the properties of solidity, liquidity, heat, movement and space respectively.

Emanation Body 'Nirmanakaya' in Sanskrit. A gross form body of a Buddha that can be seen by ordinary beings. See also *Buddha's bodies*.

Empowerment The gateway through which we enter Tantra is receiving a Tantric empowerment, which bestows upon us special blessings that heal our mental continuum and awaken our Buddha nature. When we receive a Tantric empowerment we are sowing the special seeds of the four bodies of a Buddha on our mental continuum. See *Mahamudra Tantra* and *Tantric Grounds and Paths*.

Enjoyment Body 'Sambhogakaya' in Sanskrit. A Buddha's subtle Form Body that can be perceived only by Mahayana Superiors. See also *Buddha's bodies*.

Extremes, two The extreme of existence and the extreme of non-existence. With respect to a table that appears to our mind, for example, a non-existent table is an example of an extreme of non-existence and an inherently existent table is an example of an extreme of existence. The table that we see is neither of these two extremes, so neither extreme exists. The table that we see with a valid eye consciousness exists but is empty of inherent existence.

Foe Destroyer 'Arhat' in Sanskrit. A practitioner who has abandoned all delusions and their seeds by training on the spiritual paths, and who will never again be reborn in samsara. In this context, the term 'Foe' refers to the delusions.

Form Body The Enjoyment Body and the Emanation Body of a Buddha. See also *Buddha's bodies*.

Form realm The environment of the gods who possess form and who are superior to desire realm gods. So called because the gods who inhabit it have subtle form. See *Ocean of Nectar*.

Formless realm The environment of the gods who do not possess form. See *Ocean of Nectar*.

Generic image The appearing object of a conceptual mind. The conceptual mind mistakes the generic image, or mental image, for the object itself. For example, if we think about our mother, an image of our mother appears to our conceptual mind, and it seems to that mind as if our mother herself is appearing. However, the object that principally appears to that mind is the generic image of our mother. This generic image appears to our mind through the mental exclusion of all objects that are not our mother. It is therefore the appearance of a non-non-mother. As such, like all generic images, it is a permanent phenomenon, whereas our mother herself is impermanent. See *Understanding the Mind*.

Geshe A title given by the Kadampa Monasteries to accomplished Buddhist scholars. Contracted form of the Tibetan 'ge wai she nyen', literally meaning 'virtuous friend'.

Geshe Chekhawa (AD 1102-1176) A great Kadampa Bodhisattva who composed the text *Training the Mind in Seven Points*, a commentary to Bodhisattva Langri Tangpa's *Eight Verses of Training the Mind*. He spread the study and practice of training the mind throughout Tibet. See *Universal Compassion*.

Gods Beings of the god realm, the highest of the six realms of samsara. There are many different types of god. Some are desire realm gods, while others are form or formless realm gods. See *Joyful Path of Good Fortune*.

Guide to the Bodhisattva's Way of Life A classic Mahayana Buddhist text composed by the great Indian Buddhist Yogi and scholar Shantideva, which presents all the practices of a Bodhisattva from the initial generation of bodhichitta through to the completion of the practice of the six perfections. For a translation, see *Guide to the Bodhisattva's Way of Life*. For a full commentary, see *Meaningful to Behold*.

Gungtang Gungtang Konchog Tenpai Dronme (AD 1762-1823), a Gelug scholar and meditator famous for his spiritual poems and philosophical writings.

Guru Sanskrit word for 'Spiritual Guide'. See also *Spiritual Guide*.

Hearer One of two types of Hinayana practitioner. Both Hearers and Solitary Conquerors are Hinayanists, but they differ in their motivation, behaviour, merit and wisdom. In all these respects, Solitary Conquerors are superior to Hearers. See *Ocean of Nectar*.

Hidden object An object whose initial realization by a valid cognizer depends upon correct logical reasons. See *Understanding the Mind*.

Highest Yoga Tantra The supreme quick path to enlightenment. The teachings on Highest Yoga Tantra are Buddha's ultimate intention. See *Modern Buddhism*, *Mahamudra Tantra* and *Tantric Grounds and Paths*.

Hinayana Sanskrit word for 'Lesser Vehicle'. The Hinayana goal is to attain merely one's own liberation from suffering by completely abandoning delusions. See *Joyful Path of Good Fortune*.

Impermanent phenomenon Phenomena are either permanent or impermanent. 'Impermanent' means 'momentary', thus an impermanent phenomenon is a phenomenon that is produced and disintegrates within a moment. Synonyms of impermanent phenomenon are functioning thing, thing and product.

Imprint There are two types of imprint: imprints of actions and imprints of delusions. Every action we perform leaves an imprint on the mental consciousness, and these imprints are karmic potentialities to experience certain effects in the future. The imprints left by delusions remain even after the delusions themselves have been abandoned, rather as the smell of garlic lingers in a container after the garlic has been removed. Imprints of delusions are obstructions to omniscience, and are completely abandoned only by Buddhas.

Indra A worldly god.

Ishvara A god who abides in the Land of Controlling Emanations, the highest state of existence within the desire realm. Ishvara has limited, contaminated miracle powers that make him more powerful than other beings in the desire realm. If we entrust ourself to Ishvara we may receive some temporary benefit in this life, such as an increase in wealth or possessions, but wrathful Ishvara is the enemy of those who seek liberation and he interferes with their spiritual progress. He is therefore said to be a type of Devaputra mara.

Je Tsongkhapa (AD 1357-1419) An emanation of the Wisdom Buddha Manjushri, whose appearance in fourteenth-century Tibet as a monk, and the holder of the lineage of pure view and pure deeds, was prophesied by Buddha. He spread a very pure Buddhadharma throughout Tibet, showing how to combine the practices of Sutra and Tantra, and how to practise pure Dharma during degenerate times. His tradition later became known as the 'Gelug', or 'Ganden Tradition'. See *Heart Jewel* and *Great Treasury of Merit*.

Lama Tibetan word for 'Spiritual Guide' (Skt. Guru).

Lamrim A Tibetan term, literally meaning 'stages of the path'. A special arrangement of all Buddha's teachings that is easy to understand and put into practice. It reveals all the stages of the path to enlightenment. For a full commentary, see *Joyful Path of Good Fortune*.

Land of the Thirty-three Heavens One of the six abodes of desire realm gods. See *Ocean of Nectar*.

Lineage A line of instruction that has been passed down from Spiritual Guide to disciple, with each Spiritual Guide in the line having gained personal experience of the instruction before passing it on to others.

Madhyamika A Sanskrit term, literally meaning 'Middle Way'. The higher of the two schools of Mahayana tenets. The Madhyamika view was taught by Buddha in the *Perfection of Wisdom Sutras* during the second turning of the Wheel of Dharma and was subsequently elucidated by Nagarjuna and his followers. There are two divisions of this school, Madhyamika-Svatantrika and Madhyamika-Prasangika, of which the latter is Buddha's final view. See *Meaningful to Behold* and *Ocean of Nectar*.

Mahayana Sanskrit term for 'Great Vehicle', the spiritual path to great enlightenment. The Mahayana goal is to attain Buddhahood for the benefit of all sentient beings by completely abandoning delusions and their imprints. See *Joyful Path of Good Fortune* and *Meaningful to Behold*.

Mandala offering An offering of the entire universe visualized as a Pure Land, with all its inhabitants as pure beings. See *Guide to Dakini Land* and *Great Treasury of Merit*.

Manifest object An object whose initial realization by a valid cognizer does not depend upon logical reasons. See *Understanding the Mind*.

Manjushri The embodiment of the wisdom of all the Buddhas. See *Great Treasury of Merit* and *Heart Jewel*.

Mental factor A cognizer that principally apprehends a particular attribute of an object. There are fifty-one specific mental factors. Each moment of mind comprises a primary mind and various mental factors. See *Understanding the Mind*.

Milarepa (AD 1040-1123) A great Tibetan Buddhist meditator celebrated for his beautiful songs of realization.

Mistaken mind A mind that is mistaken with respect to its appearing object. Although all minds of ordinary beings are mistaken, they are not necessarily wrong. A wrong mind is a mind that is mistaken with respect to its engaged object. Thus our eye awareness perceiving this page is a mistaken mind because the page appears as inherently existent, but it is a correct mind because it correctly apprehends the page as a page. See *Understanding the Mind*.

Naga A non-human being not normally visible to human beings. Their upper half is said to be human, their lower half serpent. Nagas usually live in the oceans of the world but they sometimes inhabit land in the region of rocks and trees. They are very powerful, some being benevolent and some malevolent. Many diseases, known as 'naga diseases', are caused by nagas and can only be cured through performing certain naga rituals.

Nalanda Monastery A great seat of Buddhist learning and practice in ancient India.

NAMO A Sanskrit word of homage and respect.

New Kadampa Tradition-International Kadampa Buddhist Union (NKT-IKBU) The union of Kadampa Buddhist Centres, an international association of study and meditation centres that follow the pure tradition of Mahayana Buddhism derived from the Buddhist meditators and scholars Atisha and Je Tsongkhapa, introduced into the West by the Buddhist teacher Venerable Geshe Kelsang Gyatso.

Non-conceptual mind A cognizer to which its object appears clearly without being mixed with a generic image. See *Understanding the Mind*.

Ordinary being Anyone who has not realized emptiness directly.

Permanent phenomenon Phenomena are either permanent or impermanent. A permanent phenomenon is a phenomenon that does not depend upon causes and that does not disintegrate moment by moment. It lacks the characteristics of production, abiding and disintegration.

Placement meditation Single-pointed concentration on a virtuous object. See *Joyful Path of Good Fortune* and *The New Meditation Handbook*.

Primary mind A cognizer that principally apprehends the mere entity of an object. Synonymous with consciousness. There are six primary minds: eye consciousness, ear consciousness, nose consciousness, tongue consciousness, body consciousness and mental consciousness. Each moment of mind comprises a primary mind and various mental factors. A primary mind and its accompanying mental factors are the same entity but have different functions. See *Understanding the Mind*.

Pure Land A pure environment in which there are no true sufferings. There are many Pure Lands. For example, Tushita is the Pure Land of Buddha Maitreya, Sukhavati is the Pure Land of Buddha Amitabha, and Dakini Land, or Keajra, is the Pure Land of Buddha Vajrayogini and Buddha Heruka. See *Living Meaningfully, Dying Joyfully*.

Saraha One of the first Mahasiddhas, and the Teacher of Nagarjuna. See *Essence of Vajrayana*.

Sentient being Any being who possesses a mind that is contaminated by delusions or their imprints. Both 'sentient being' and 'living being' are terms used to distinguish beings whose minds are contaminated by either of these two obstructions from Buddhas, whose minds are completely free from these obstructions.

Shantideva (AD 687-763) A great Indian Buddhist scholar and meditation master. He composed *Guide to the Bodhisattva's Way of Life*. See *Meaningful to Behold* and *Guide to the Bodhisattva's Way of Life*.

Shariputra One of Buddha Shakyamuni's principal disciples. He has the aspect of a Hinayana Foe Destroyer.

Solitary Conqueror One of two types of Hinayana practitioner. Also known as 'Solitary Realizer'. See also *Hearer*.

Spiritual Guide 'Guru' in Sanskrit, 'Lama' in Tibetan. A Teacher who guides us along the spiritual path. See *Joyful Path of Good Fortune* and *Great Treasury of Merit*.

Tantra Synonymous with Secret Mantra. Tantric teachings are distinguished from Sutra teachings in that they reveal methods for training the mind by bringing the future result, or Buddhahood, into the present path. Tantric practitioners overcome ordinary appearances and conceptions by visualizing their body, environment, enjoyments and deeds as those of a Buddha. Tantra is the supreme path to full enlightenment. Tantric practices are to be done in private and only by those who have received a Tantric empowerment. See *Modern Buddhism*, *Tantric Grounds and Paths* and *Mahamudra Tantra*.

Ten directions The four cardinal directions, the four intermediate directions, and the directions above and below.

Training the mind A special lineage of instructions that came from Buddha Shakyamuni through Manjushri and Shantideva to Atisha and the Kadampa Geshes, which emphasizes the generation of bodhichitta through the practices of equalizing and exchanging self with others combined with taking and giving. Known as 'lojong' in Tibetan. See *Universal Compassion, Eight Steps to Happiness* and *Modern Buddhism*.

Tranquil abiding A concentration that possesses the special bliss of physical and mental suppleness that is attained in dependence upon completing the nine mental abidings. See *Joyful Path of Good Fortune* and *Meaningful to Behold*.

Trijang Rinpoche, Dorjechang (AD 1901-1981) A special Tibetan Lama of the twentieth century who was an emanation of Buddha Shakyamuni, Heruka, Atisha, Amitabha and Je Tsongkhapa. Also known as 'Kyabje Trijang Rinpoche' and 'Losang Yeshe'.

Truth Body See *Buddha's bodies*.

Two obstructions Obstructions to liberation and obstructions to omniscience. Hinayana Foe Destroyers and Bodhisattvas above the seventh ground have abandoned the obstructions to liberation but not the obstructions to omniscience. Consequently, when they are not in meditative equipoise on emptiness, objects appear to them as inherently existent.

Vajra Generally, the Sanskrit word 'vajra' means indestructible like a diamond and powerful like a thunderbolt. It is also the name given to a metal ritual object. See *Tantric Grounds and Paths*.

Vajra posture The perfect cross-legged posture. See *Joyful Path of Good Fortune*.

Vajradhara The founder of Vajrayana, or Tantra. He appears directly only to highly realized Bodhisattvas to whom he gives Tantric teachings. To benefit other living beings with less merit, he manifested in the more visible form of Buddha Shakyamuni. He also said that in degenerate times he would appear in an ordinary form as a Spiritual Guide. See *Great Treasury of Merit*.

Very subtle mind There are different levels of mind: gross, subtle and very subtle. Subtle minds manifest when the inner winds gather and dissolve within the central channel. See *Clear Light of Bliss* and *Mahamudra Tantra*.

Wheel of Dharma A collection of Buddha's teachings. Buddha gave his teachings in three main phases, which are known as 'the three turnings of the Wheel of Dharma'. During the first Wheel he taught the four noble truths, during the second he taught the *Perfection of Wisdom Sutras* and revealed the Madhyamika-Prasangika view, and during the third he taught the Chittamatra view. These teachings were given according to the inclinations and dispositions of his disciples. Buddha's final view is that of the second Wheel.

Wisdom Truth Body See also *Buddha's bodies*

Bibliography

Geshe Kelsang Gyatso is a highly respected meditation master and scholar of the Mahayana Buddhist tradition founded by Je Tsongkhapa. Since arriving in the West in 1977, Geshe Kelsang has worked tirelessly to establish pure Buddhadharma throughout the world. Over this period he has given extensive teachings on the major scriptures of the Mahayana. These teachings provide a comprehensive presentation of the essential Sutra and Tantra practices of Mahayana Buddhism.

Books

The following books by Geshe Kelsang are all published by Tharpa Publications.

The Bodhisattva Vow A practical guide to helping others. (2nd. edn., 1995)

Clear Light of Bliss A Tantric meditation manual. (2nd. edn., 1992)

Eight Steps to Happiness The Buddhist way of loving kindness. (2nd. edn., 2012)

Essence of Vajrayana The Highest Yoga Tantra practice of Heruka body mandala. (1997)

Great Treasury of Merit How to rely upon a Spiritual Guide. (1992)

Guide to the Bodhisattva's Way of Life How to enjoy a life of great meaning and altruism. (A translation of Shantideva's famous verse masterpiece.) (2002)

Heart Jewel The essential practices of Kadampa Buddhism. (2nd. edn., 1997)

How to Solve Our Human Problems The four noble truths. (2005)

Introduction to Buddhism An explanation of the Buddhist way of life. (2nd. edn., 2001)

Joyful Path of Good Fortune The complete Buddhist path to enlightenment. (2nd. edn., 1995)

Living Meaningfully, Dying Joyfully The profound practice of transference of consciousness. (1999)

Mahamudra Tantra The supreme Heart Jewel nectar. (2005)

Meaningful to Behold The Bodhisattva's way of life. (5th. edn., 2007)

Modern Buddhism The Path of Compassion and Wisdom. (2011)

The New Guide to Dakini Land The Highest Yoga Tantra practice of Buddha Vajrayogini. (3rd. edn., 2012)

The New Heart of Wisdom Profound teachings from Buddha's Heart (An explanation of the *Heart Sutra*). (5th. edn., 2012)

The New Meditation Handbook Meditations to make our life happy and meaningful. (4th. edn., 2003)

Ocean of Nectar The true nature of all things. (1995)

Tantric Grounds and Paths How to enter, progress on, and complete the Vajrayana path. (1994)

Transform Your Life A blissful journey. (2001)

Understanding the Mind The nature and power of the mind. (3rd. edn., 2002)

Universal Compassion Inspiring solutions for difficult times. (4th. edn., 2002)

Sadhanas and Other Booklets

Geshe Kelsang has also supervised the translation of a collection of essential sadhanas, or ritual prayers for spiritual attainments, available in booklet or audio formats.

Avalokiteshvara Sadhana Prayers and requests to the Buddha of Compassion.

The Blissful Path The condensed self-generation sadhana of Vajrayogini.

The Bodhisattva's Confession of Moral Downfalls The purification practice of the *Mahayana Sutra of the Three Superior Heaps.*

Condensed Essence of Vajrayana Condensed Heruka body mandala self-generation sadhana.

Dakini Yoga The middling self-generation sadhana of Vajrayogini.

Drop of Essential Nectar A special fasting and purification practice in conjunction with Eleven-faced Avalokiteshvara.

Essence of Good Fortune Prayers for the six preparatory practices for meditation on the stages of the path to enlightenment.

Essence of Vajrayana Heruka body mandala self-generation sadhana according to the system of Mahasiddha Ghantapa.

Feast of Great Bliss Vajrayogini self-initiation sadhana.

Great Liberation of the Father Preliminary prayers for Mahamudra meditation in conjunction with Heruka practice.

Great Liberation of the Mother Preliminary prayers for Mahamudra meditation in conjunction with Vajrayogini practice.

The Great Mother A method to overcome hindrances and obstacles by reciting the *Essence of Wisdom Sutra* (the *Heart Sutra*).

A Handbook for the Daily Practice of Bodhisattva Vows and Tantric Vows.

Heartfelt Prayers Funeral service for cremations and burials.

Heart Jewel The Guru yoga of Je Tsongkhapa combined with the condensed sadhana of his Dharma Protector.

The Kadampa Way of Life The essential practice of Kadam Lamrim.

Liberation from Sorrow Praises and requests to the Twenty-one Taras.

Mahayana Refuge Ceremony and Bodhisattva Vow Ceremony.

Medicine Buddha Prayer A method for benefiting others.

Medicine Buddha Sadhana A method for accomplishing the attainments of Medicine Buddha.

Meditation and Recitation of Solitary Vajrasattva.

Melodious Drum Victorious in all Directions The extensive fulfilling and restoring ritual of the Dharma Protector, the great king Dorje Shugden, in conjunction with Mahakala, Kalarupa, Kalindewi and other Dharma Protectors.

Offering to the Spiritual Guide (Lama Chopa) A special way of relying upon a Spiritual Guide.

Path of Compassion for the Deceased Powa sadhana for the benefit of the deceased.

Pathway to the Pure Land Training in powa – the transference of consciousness.

Powa Ceremony Transference of consciousness for the deceased.

Prayers for Meditation Brief preparatory prayers for meditation.

Prayers for World Peace.

A Pure Life The practice of taking and keeping the eight Mahayana precepts.

Quick Path to Great Bliss The extensive self-generation sadhana of Vajrayogini.

The Root Tantra of Heruka and Vajrayogini Chapters One & Fifty-one of the *Condensed Heruka Root Tantra*.

The Root Text: Eight Verses of Training the Mind.

Treasury of Wisdom The sadhana of Venerable Manjushri.

The Uncommon Yoga of Inconceivability The special instruction of how to reach the Pure Land of Keajra with this human body.

Union of No More Learning Heruka body mandala self-initiation sadhana.

Vajra Hero Yoga The brief practice of Heruka body mandala self-generation.

The Vows and Commitments of Kadampa Buddhism.

Wishfulfilling Jewel The Guru yoga of Je Tsongkhapa combined with the sadhana of his Dharma Protector.

The Yoga of Buddha Amitayus A special method for increasing lifespan, wisdom and merit.

The Yoga of Buddha Heruka The essential self-generation sadhana of Heruka body mandala & Condensed six-session yoga.

The Yoga of Buddha Maitreya Self-generation sadhana.

The Yoga of Buddha Vajrapani Self-generation sadhana.

The Yoga of Enlightened Mother Arya Tara Self-generation sadhana.

The Yoga of Great Mother Prajnaparamita Self-generation sadhana.

The Yoga of Thousand-armed Avalokiteshvara Self-generation sadhana.

The Yoga of White Tara, Buddha of Long Life.

To order any of our publications, or to request a catalogue, please visit www.tharpa.com or contact your nearest Tharpa Office listed on page 327.

NKT – IKBU

Study Programmes of Kadampa Buddhism

Kadampa Buddhism is a Mahayana Buddhist school founded by the great Indian Buddhist Master Atisha (AD 982-1054). His followers are known as 'Kadampas'. 'Ka' means 'word' and refers to Buddha's teachings, and 'dam' refers to Atisha's special Lamrim instructions known as 'the stages of the path to enlightenment'. By integrating their knowledge of all Buddha's teachings into their practice of Lamrim, and by integrating this into their everyday lives, Kadampa Buddhists are encouraged to use Buddha's teachings as practical methods for transforming daily activities into the path to enlightenment. The great Kadampa Teachers are famous not only for being great scholars, but also for being spiritual practitioners of immense purity and sincerity.

The lineage of these teachings, both their oral transmission and blessings, was then passed from Teacher to disciple, spreading throughout much of Asia, and now to many countries throughout the Western world. Buddha's teachings, which are known as 'Dharma', are likened to a wheel that moves from country to country in accordance with changing conditions and people's karmic inclinations. The external forms of presenting Buddhism may change as it meets with different cultures and societies, but its essential authenticity is ensured through the continuation of an unbroken lineage of realized practitioners.

Kadampa Buddhism was first introduced into the West in 1977 by the renowned Buddhist Master, Venerable Geshe Kelsang Gyatso. Since that time, he has worked tirelessly to spread Kadampa Buddhism throughout the world by giving extensive teachings, writing many profound texts on Kadampa Buddhism, and founding the New Kadampa Tradition – International Kadampa Buddhist Union (NKT-IKBU), which now has over a thousand Kadampa Buddhist Centres and groups worldwide. Each Centre offers study programmes on Buddhist psychology, philosophy and meditation instruction, as well as retreats for all levels of practitioner. The emphasis is on integrating Buddha's teachings into daily life to solve our human problems and to spread lasting peace and happiness throughout the world.

The Kadampa Buddhism of the NKT-IKBU is an entirely independent Buddhist tradition and has no political affiliations. It is an association of Buddhist Centres and practitioners that derive their inspiration and guidance from the example of the ancient Kadampa Buddhist Masters and their teachings, as presented by Geshe Kelsang.

There are three reasons why we need to study and practise the teachings of Buddha: to develop our wisdom, to cultivate a good heart, and to maintain a peaceful state of mind. If we do not strive to develop our wisdom, we will always remain ignorant of ultimate truth – the true nature of reality. Although we wish for happiness, our ignorance leads us to engage in non-virtuous actions, which are the main cause of all our suffering. If we do not cultivate a good heart, our selfish motivation destroys harmony and good relationships with others. We have no peace, and no chance to gain pure happiness. Without inner peace, outer peace is impossible. If we do not maintain a peaceful state of mind, we are not happy even if we have ideal conditions. On the other hand, when our mind is peaceful, we are happy, even if our external conditions are unpleasant. Therefore, the development of these qualities is of utmost importance for our daily happiness.

Geshe Kelsang Gyatso, or 'Geshe-la' as he is affectionately called by his students, has designed three special spiritual programmes for the systematic study and practice of Kadampa Buddhism that are especially suited to the modern world – the General Programme (GP), the Foundation Programme (FP) and the Teacher Training Programme (TTP).

GENERAL PROGRAMME

The General Programme provides a basic introduction to Buddhist view, meditation and practice that is suitable for beginners. It also includes advanced teachings and practice from both Sutra and Tantra.

FOUNDATION PROGRAMME

The Foundation Programme provides an opportunity to deepen our understanding and experience of Buddhism through a systematic study of six texts:

1 *Joyful Path of Good Fortune* – a commentary to Atisha's Lamrim instructions, the stages of the path to enlightenment.
2 *Universal Compassion* – a commentary to Bodhisattva Chekhawa's *Training the Mind in Seven Points*.
3 *Eight Steps to Happiness* – a commentary to Bodhisattva Langri Tangpa's *Eight Verses of Training the Mind*.
4 *The New Heart of Wisdom* – a commentary to the *Heart Sutra*.

5 *Meaningful to Behold* – a commentary to Venerable Shantideva's *Guide to the Bodhisattva's Way of Life*.

6 *Understanding the Mind* – a detailed explanation of the mind, based on the works of the Buddhist scholars Dharmakirti and Dignaga.

The benefits of studying and practising these texts are as follows:

(1) *Joyful Path of Good Fortune* – we gain the ability to put all Buddha's teachings of both Sutra and Tantra into practice. We can easily make progress on, and complete, the stages of the path to the supreme happiness of enlightenment. From a practical point of view, Lamrim is the main body of Buddha's teachings, and the other teachings are like its limbs.

(2) and (3) *Universal Compassion* and *Eight Steps to Happiness* – we gain the ability to integrate Buddha's teachings into our daily life and solve all our human problems.

(4) *The New Heart of Wisdom* – we gain a realization of the ultimate nature of reality. By gaining this realization, we can eliminate the ignorance of self-grasping, which is the root of all our suffering.

(5) *Meaningful to Behold* – we transform our daily activities into the Bodhisattva's way of life, thereby making every moment of our human life meaningful.

(6) *Understanding the Mind* – we understand the relationship between our mind and its external objects. If we understand that objects depend upon the subjective mind, we can change the way objects appear to us by changing our own mind. Gradually, we will gain the ability to control our mind and in this way solve all our problems.

TEACHER TRAINING PROGRAMME

The Teacher Training Programme is designed for people who wish to train as authentic Dharma Teachers. In addition to completing the study of fourteen texts of Sutra and Tantra, which include the six texts mentioned above, the student is required to observe certain commitments with regard to behaviour and way of life, and to complete a number of meditation retreats.

A Special Teacher Training Programme is also held at Kadampa Meditation Centres in certain city commercial spaces. This includes a special meditation and study programme that focuses on the following five books: *Modern Buddhism*, *The New Heart of Wisdom*, *The New Guide to Dakini Land*, *Joyful Path of Good Fortune* and *Meaningful to Behold*, the commentary to Shantideva's *Guide to the Bodhisattva's Way of Life*.

All Kadampa Buddhist Centres are open to the public. Every year we celebrate Festivals in many countries throughout the world, including two in England, where people gather from around the world to receive special teachings and empowerments and to enjoy a spiritual holiday. Please feel free to visit us at any time!

For further information about NKT-IKBU study programmes or to find your nearest centre, visit www.kadampa.org, or contact:

NKT-IKBU Central Office
Conishead Priory, Ulverston
Cumbria, LA12 9QQ, UK
Tel: +44 (0)1229-588533
Fax: +44 (0)1229-587775
Email: info@kadampa.org
Website: www.kadampa.org

or:

US NKT-IKBU Office
Kadampa Meditation Center
47 Sweeney Road, Glen Spey,
NY 12737, USA
Tel: +1 845-856-9000
Toll-free: + 888-741-3475
Fax: +1 845-856-2110
Email: info@nkt-kmc-newyork.org
Website: www.nkt-kmc-newyork.org

Tharpa Offices Worldwide

Tharpa books are currently published in English (UK and US), Chinese, French, German, Italian, Japanese, Portuguese and Spanish. Most languages are available from any Tharpa office listed below.

UK Office

Tharpa Publications UK
Conishead Priory
ULVERSTON
Cumbria, LA12 9QQ, UK
Tel: +44 (0)1229-588599
Fax: +44 (0)1229-483919
Web: www.tharpa.com/uk/
E-mail: info.uk@tharpa.com

US Office

Tharpa Publications USA
47 Sweeney Road
GLEN SPEY NY 12737, USA
Tel: +1 845-856-5102
Toll-free: 888-741-3475
Fax: +1 845-856-2110
Web: www.tharpa.com/us/
E-mail: info.us@tharpa.com

Asian Office

Tharpa Asia
Zhong Zheng E Rd, Sec 2,
Lane 143, Alley 10, No 7,
Tamsui District, NEW TAIPEI
CITY, 25159, TAIWAN
Tel: +886-(02)-8809-4313
Web: www.tharpa.com/hk-en/
E-mail: info.asia@tharpa.com

Australian Office

Tharpa Publications Australia
25 McCarthy Road (PO Box 63)
MONBULK VIC 3793
AUSTRALIA
Tel: +61 (0)3 9752-0377
Web: www.tharpa.com/au/
E-mail: info.au@tharpa.com

Brazilian Office

Editora Tharpa Brasil
Rua Fradique Coutinho 701
VILA MADALENA
05416-011 São Paulo - SP
BRAZIL
Tel/Fax: +55 (11) 3812 7509
Web: www.tharpa.com.br
E-mail: contato@tharpa.com.br

Canadian Office

Tharpa Publications Canada
631 Crawford St., TORONTO
ON M6G 3K1, CANADA
Tel: +1 416-762-8710
Toll-free: 866-523-2672
Fax: +1 416-762-2267
Web: www.tharpa.com/ca/
E-mail: info.ca@tharpa.com

French Office
Editions Tharpa
Château de Segrais
72220 SAINT-MARS-OUTILLÉ
FRANCE
Tel : +33 (0)2 43 87 71 02
Fax : +33 (0)2 76 01 34 10
Web: www.tharpa.com/fr/
E-mail: info.fr@tharpa.com

German Office
Tharpa-Verlag
Sommerswalde 8
16727 OBERKRÄMER
GERMANY
Tel: +49 (033055) 222 135
Fax : +49 (033055) 222 139
Web: www.tharpa.com/de/
E-mail: info.de@tharpa.com

Japanese Office
Tharpa Japan
c/o Kazuko Numata,
Amitabha Buddhist Centre,
Shimagahara 11399-35, IGA- SHI,
Mie 519-1711, JAPAN
Tel/Fax: +81 (0)595-59-2008
Web: www.meditationinjapan.com
E-mail: info.jp@tharpa.com

Mexican Office
Enrique Rébsamen No 406,
Col. Narvate, entre Xola y
Diagonal de San Antonio, C.P.
03020, MÉXICO D.F., MÉXICO
Tel: +01 (55) 56 39 61 86
Tel/Fax: +01 (55) 56 39 61 80
Web: www.tharpa.com/mx/
E-mail: tharpa@kadampa.org.mx

South African Office
c/o Mahasiddha Kadampa
Buddhist Centre
2 Hollings Road, Malvern
DURBAN 4093
REP. OF SOUTH AFRICA
Tel : +27 (0)31 464 0984
Fax: +27 (0)86 513 3476
Web: www.tharpa.com/za/
E-mail: info.za@tharpa.com

Spanish Office
Editorial Tharpa España
Camino Fuente del Perro s/n
29120 ALHAURÍN EL
GRANDE (Málaga), SPAIN
Tel.: +34 952 596808
Fax: +34 952 490175
Web: www.tharpa.com/es/
E-mail: info.es@tharpa.com

Swiss Office
Tharpa Verlag AG
Mirabellenstrasse 1
CH-8048 ZÜRICH
SWITZERLAND
Tel: +41 44 401 02 20
Fax: +41 44 461 36 88
Web: www.tharpa.com/ch/
E-mail: info.ch@tharpa.com

Index

The letter 'g' indicates an entry in the glossary